PRAISE FOR
ANYTIME PLAYDATE

"Dade Hayes was granted extraordinary access to the people who create that mesmerizing TV your young kids can't take their eyes off. *Anytime Playdate* is a behind-the-scenes look at an industry—and yes, it is an industry—that makes money by entertaining children too young to speak in full sentences. Entertaining and informative at the same time, it's a quick read that you can digest while your child naps or plays nearby (that's when I read it!)."

—Jean Twenge, Ph.D., author of *Generation Me*

"With *Anytime Playdate*, Dade Hayes has provided us all with a fascinating and entertaining look at the power of preschool TV programming. Not only is it changing how I talk with parents about structuring their home lives, it's changing how I structure my own."

—Hal Runkel, author of *Screamfree Parenting*
and creator of screamfree.com

"A full-frontal view of the origins and business end of children's television, from *Howdy Doody* and *Sesame Street* through *Blue's Clues* to new shows our kids haven't even become addicted to yet . . . If you've ever left your kid in front of the TV set for more than the time it takes to say 'I love you. You love me,' you need to read this book."

—Robert Wilder, author of *Daddy Needs a Drink*
and *Tales from the Teachers' Lounge*

_f_**P**

ALSO BY DADE HAYES

Open Wide:
How Hollywood Box Office Became a National Obsession
(co-written with Jonathan Bing)

ANYTIME PLAYDATE

Inside the Preschool
Entertainment Boom,

or

How Television Became
My Baby's Best Friend

Dade Hayes

Free Press
New York London Toronto Sydney

FREE PRESS
A Division of Simon & Schuster, Inc.
1230 Avenue of the Americas
New York, NY 10020

First Free Press hardcover edition April 2008

FREE PRESS and colophon are trademarks of Simon & Schuster, Inc.

For information about special discounts for bulk purchases, please contact Simon & Schuster Special Sales at 1-800-456-6798 or business@simonandschuster.com

Manufactured in the United States of America

10   9   8   7   6   5   4   3   2   1

Library of Congress Cataloging-in-Publication Data

Hayes, Dade.
Anytime playdate: inside the preschool entertainment boom, or, how television became my baby's best friend / by Dade Hayes.
p.   cm.
Includes bibliographical references and index.
1. Television programs for children—United States.   2. Television and children—United States.   I. Title.
PN1992.8.C46H39   2008
302.23'45083—dc22   2007046177

ISBN-13: 978-1-4165-4683-2
ISBN-10:   1-4165-4683-9

To Stella, Margot, and Finley,
moon and stars

CONTENTS

Contents

ANYTIME
PLAYDATE

1

THE ACTIVE VIEWING
REVOLUTION IS HERE

The family television set, a twenty-seven-inch Toshiba, suddenly seemed to loom over the living room with the omniscient aura of the monolith in *2001*. For reasons I am still trying to understand, I cocked my head that winter morning, apelike, and beheld it as a mysterious gift from the technology gods. This was no longer a mere hunk of metal and glass on which I squandered my own waking hours, watching three consecutive *SportsCenters* or handicapping which sequined pair would win *Dancing with the Stars*. No, this cube was now a Socratic learning tool, even a shamanistic guide to life. And I, as father and provider, would bestow it upon my daughter, who would bask in its radiant, edifying glow for all her days. Margot was six months old at the time. And it's worth noting that my epiphany occurred at 6:17 A.M.

The morning shift had become my routine once Margot had blessedly learned to sleep through the night. I rose with her as a small trade-off for the fact that my wife, Stella, usually put her down to sleep and awakened for multiple nighttime feedings.

Coping with the skull-scrambling feeling of new-parent jet lag, I would retrieve the newspaper, hold Margot close to my bathrobe-clad body, and shuffle downstairs. Lurching Tony Soprano–style into the kitchen, I'd balance her over one shoulder while I ground coffee beans, measured out water, started a pot brewing, and warmed up her breakfast. On that fateful morning, we plopped down in the living room on a floor mat known by its marketers as the Tiny Love Gymini® 3D Activity Gym. Tiny Love claims that its red, white, and black geometric design approximates the womb and stimulates babies' brains. I can't speak for Margot, but the mat apparently made a synapse fire in my head, and I remembered a TV program I had not seen for almost thirty years. I sparked up the Toshiba and tuned to *Sesame Street*.

An hour passed blissfully. We sat together but faced the screen. I read the paper and slurped my coffee, glancing up occasionally to see reassuringly familiar sights straight out of my own childhood: the classic New York stoops, Big Bird talking to Maria, Oscar in his trash can. Margot cooed and pointed a couple of times, especially during a computer-animated segment that was new to me, "Elmo's World." I couldn't tell exactly what she made of *Sesame Street*, but I took great comfort in that hour. It was me-time that doubled as an introduction for her to some of my old friends, who, I believed, would teach her only the purest principles, the most intellect-enhancing concepts—Tiny Love on the floor, tiny love on the screen.

Of course things did not remain so simple. Day after day of this morning ritual (often repeated in the evenings as we made dinner) soon got Margot hooked. She would gaze, gape-mouthed, for up to two hours at a shot. Attempting to turn the TV off became an ordeal that produced tears and screams. Over the next few months, as she grew, the menu of offerings seemed to expand accordingly. A modest serving of *Sesame Street* exploded into a twenty-four-hour Las Vegas buffet of diversions. Between DVD and cable TV, dozens of playmates beckoned and Margot fell in with a rotating series of them, most with short, catchy names— Maisy, Miffy, Oobi, Franklin, JoJo, Caillou, Dora. When her obsession became the low-rent DVD series called *Baby Prodigy*, starring a duck named Dookie ("Raise a healthier, smarter baby!" the box blares), it seemed there was no end to the offerings. I felt like I was trapped in the final shot of *Raiders of the Lost Ark*, a long zoom-out that reveals not just the single, known ark in a crate but a vast, Orwellian warehouse of goods.

The journalist part of me stirred. I wanted to find out more about the supply side of the preschool entertainment equation, rather than just participating in it as a parent eager for a glimpse at the morning paper and a vestige of my preparenthood routine. Looking closer, I was astounded by how massive the warehouse was and how meticulously and secretly its contents were calibrated to stoke the appetites of consumers barely able to sit up.

As I started exploring the boom, quotidian objects and names I took for granted suddenly acquired startling new dimensions. Take Tiny Love, an Israeli company that has rapidly expanded well beyond its traditional business of mats and rattles. It is now pushing a video series called *MagIQ* designed for kids from six to thirty-six months. A company spokesman hastened to insist that Tiny Love "wasn't much into sitting a baby down in front of a DVD and letting them just be a couch potato." Therefore, in order to engender more interactivity, the company packaged the DVDs, which show simple animations of boats, ducks, and the like, with a little stuffed teddy bear. The bear comes with a chip inside and a series of vocal responses to what's playing on the screen. According to the company and the "experts" it marshaled, the presence of the bear creates more interaction with the child and the screen.

The promotional video for *MagIQ* speaks volumes. "A ball," the narrator begins as everyday objects appear on-screen. "Your baby can kick it, pass it, chase it. A butterfly. Your baby can play with it, sing to it, make friends with it. A xylophone. Listen to it. Dance to it. Make awful noise to it. An apple. Eat it. Wash it. Roll it. Color. Paint it. Express himself with it. But when all this appears on a TV screen, your baby can only . . . watch it." Cut to a shot of a two-year-old in a beanbag chair looking at a TV with raccoon eyes and a frown. "That's why Tiny Love has decided to create *MagIQ*." A choir sings: "Maaaa-giiic!" The narrator continues, "A totally active new viewing experience that makes your baby switch from passive to active. The magic lies within the triangle formed by your baby, the TV, and our truly special doll. Our doll encourages your baby to participate, sing, laugh, and react to the DVD content on the screen."

A voice on the screen-within-the-screen says, "I see—the boat is upside down!" and the camera shows a baby looking between her legs, upside down, and laughing. A montage follows showing babies smiling and laughing as the elemental animations play on the room's TV screen. The background is completely white. White furniture, white walls. Are we in heaven?

"So next time you buy a DVD for your baby, don't just watch the screen. Watch your baby. And if she looks like this [a smash-cut montage shows laughing one-year-olds playing with the doll] then it must be MagIQ. The active viewing revolution is here."

Actively or passively, preschoolers devour $21 billion worth of TV programs, DVDs, CDs, stage shows, magazines, and tie-in toys every year—a figure that has nearly tripled since 2001. In that watershed year, the Walt Disney Company bought the Baby Einstein line of DVDs and toys and *Dora the Explorer* went on the air. *Dora* now generates $1.5 billion in annual revenue and draws nine million viewers each morning, more than *Today* or *Good Morning America*. A recent survey by nonprofit group Zero to Three found that the mean age when babies start watching videos is 6.1 months and they watch television at 9.8 months. Baby Einstein, acquired for $25 million, has mushroomed into a billion-dollar asset that cranks out a spectrum of "infant development" products from videos to bassinets to party kits. Dozens of companies emulating those top brands have collectively altered child-rearing by marketing to viewers from an age they chillingly call "zero," though the real targets are their doting, gear-obsessed parents, the first TV-raised generation to become parents themselves. These new parents have scooped up millions of CDs by artists such as Dan Zanes, the former lead singer of '80s college-rock band the Del Fuegos who has reinvented himself as the floppy-haired Pied Piper of preschool kids. They have laughed along with spoofs of their Muppet-TV youth such as Broadway's *Avenue Q* or MTV2's lacerating *Wonder Showzen,* whose creators' stated aim is to "take all the things you loved about watching TV as a kid and turn them into a twisted nightmare for all ages."

The airwaves teem with preschool TV networks, among them Noggin, PBS Kids Sprout, BabyFirstTV (aimed, incredibly, at children ages six to thirty-six months), BabyTV, and large blocks of programming on Cartoon Network, the Disney Channel, Discovery Channel, and The Learning Channel. A generation ago, there were two shows for preschoolers: *Sesame Street* and *Mister*

Rogers' Neighborhood. Today, more than fifty shows vie for the two- to five-year-old audience every day of the week. Thriving DVD lines such as *Baby Einstein, Baby Genius,* and *Brainy Baby* are among many targeting the very youngest viewers with a cognitive development bent. Sesame Workshop has drawn protests from some child development advocates with its new infant DVDs called *Sesame Beginnings,* which use diaper-clad baby versions of Elmo, Big Bird, and Cookie Monster to reach under-twos and their parents. By 2007, one in three DVDs bought in the United States (51 million units) was intended for the pacifier crowd.

Nielsen, the TV ratings company, has no reliable method of tracking viewers under two years old, and scientific research is scarce and inconclusive as to the effects of media exposure on them. "They're very squirrelly and you have to infer what they're thinking," explained Georgene Troseth, a preschool media expert at Vanderbilt University. Yet this audience is clearly fueling the boom. A 2006 study found that 59 percent of kids under two watch TV daily; 42 percent begin watching before they turn one; 36 percent have TV sets in their own room; and 52 percent know how to operate the remote control. U.S. population trends are likely to accelerate the flow of product into the marketplace—the U.S. Census Bureau projects the annual birth rate to grow by 20 percent over the next generation, from 4 million now to 4.8 million in 2028.

How exactly do conglomerates target the ultrayoung? Are they pushing ethical boundaries to do so? And what happens on the receiving end of the transaction—in the living room, where the marketing messages and parental choices are made manifest? That is what this book intends to explore.

As I looked around and started to take stock of the glut and the need for shows to compete by proclaiming their idiosyncrasies, I quickly realized that the monoculture of *Sesame Street, Mister Rogers,* and *Captain Kangaroo* had disappeared. The shows I watched as a toddler tapped into shared notions of child development and entertainment with a sunny mix of alphabet games, live-action footage of kids, and puppet fantasies. In today's fragmented mediascape, targeted messages are much more essential. There are entire networks whose preschool philosophies involve the use of humor (Cartoon Network) or the importance of optimism (Discovery Kids). There are "play-to-learn" shows built on physical gags and unadorned fun (*Wow! Wow! Wubbzy!*), shows with math or science orientation (*Peep and the Big Wide World*), "preliteracy" shows (*Between the Lions, Super Why!*), live-action performance shows (*The Doodlebops, Hi-5*), hip-hop-flavored shows (*Hip Hop Harry, Yo Gabba Gabba!*), and shows whose main attribute is animation achieved by computers or the more old-fashioned means of clay or pencils. Noggin, one of the networks solely dedicated to preschool fare, even claims its broadcast day is designed around the elements of a day in preschool (circle time, snack time, show and tell, and so on), with a diversified programming slate to match.

Brown Johnson, president of Nickelodeon Preschool and a key figure in the success of shows such as *Dora* and *Blue's Clues,* believes the sheer number of options available today is a good thing. "More is always better for the audience," she told me. "A lot of people are trying to get in on it. Kids over six don't buy toys; they're turning to technology. They don't buy dolls, they don't buy plush. The toy market has gone 'pfft.' Commercially, people are trying to make that pay. Hits are hits in the preschool space, but you can count them on one hand: *Sesame Street, Blue's Clues, Dora.* . . . Disney is making some great stuff and they're pouring more into making a hit."

After a pause, she expanded her business analysis to the broader society, adding, "There's another side to it, and that is that parents are just really busy. The median income of a household with kids is forty-eight thousand dollars. Sixty-five percent of moms work outside the home. Parents are under a lot of stress. I feel like we need to provide quality entertainment for the broadest possible access in order to support parents." Rosemarie Truglio, head of research for Sesame Workshop, echoed Johnson's point. "Adults are living a faster-paced, highly stressed time," she said. "So when they saw something that was something that did not involve them [i.e., television], they welcomed it. Past generations had a little more time, so there wasn't the same speed of adoption of media."

The debate about content invariably ends up back in the living room. The role of parents is an x factor that is nearly impossible for researchers to account for in their studies. Truglio and others are pushing for more ethnographic research that would take into account the environment of the home where media is consumed. As it stands now, most people look only at consumption and the only question that seems to resonate is, "Is the television on or off?"

"You can watch the world's worst programming," Johnson said, "but if your parent is sitting next to you saying, 'Oh my God, can you believe they make girls look like that?' or 'Oh my God, why don't they talk to each other instead of shooting at each other?' then it can do something positive."

Johnson was describing something that the industry terms "co-viewing," a shared experience between parent and child in which helping children process what is on-screen is a goal for the parent. The notion blossomed with the multimedia phenomenon *Free to Be ... You & Me,* a project that sought to offer kids and their parents stories and folk tales that upended old gender and racial stereotypes. Marlo Thomas and Gloria Steinem originated the concept as an album featuring a who's who of guest contributors, from Mel Brooks and Carl Reiner to Diana Ross and Shel Silverstein. It then became a bestselling book, then a TV special, and, eventually, a play. At its center was the shared experience of entertainment, with the goal of parents and children benefiting equally.

In order to fully consider the potential for co-viewing, it is important to remember civilization's long reluctance even to acknowledge childhood as a distinct developmental phase. As recently as the mid-19th century, children were sent to work in factories when they might otherwise enter kindergarten, and no one ever celebrated their birthdays. The late critic Neil Postman argued that American culture in recent decades has been returning to a state of fundamental hostility toward the idea of childhood, albeit via a less physically taxing route. Instead of dispatching children into Dickensian mines, parents today are placing children on a hyperaccelerated track at an alarmingly early juncture in life.

Why? Guilt, Postman wrote, citing Enlightenment philosopher John Locke. In works such as his 1693 book *Some Thoughts Concerning Education,* Locke portrayed the child mind as a blank slate, or *tabula rasa.* "Like Freud's ideas about psychic repression two hundred years later, Locke's *tabula rasa* created a sense of guilt in parents about their child's development," Postman wrote in his seminal book, *The Disappearance of Childhood,* "and provided the psychological and epistemological grounds for making the careful nurturing of children a national priority." There has also long been an inherent conflict for parents about the degree to which they should expose children to the complexities of the real world. William Blake's *Songs of Innocence* and *Songs of Experience,* illustrated companion books of poems published in the late

9

18th century, examine that loaded issue. In *Innocence,* the poems position pain and cruelty as forces held at bay by mother and father, who seek to preserve the innocence of the child. In *Experience,* the darkness descends and the world's ills can no longer be contained. One poem's narrator, in recalling her childhood, "turns green and pale" as children play nearby.

By the middle decades of the 20th century, amid the emergence of electronic media as a social force, child development pioneers Jean Piaget and Lev Vygotsky had each advanced the notion of young children's growth occurring in distinct stages. Piaget in particular wrote voluminously and vividly about the experiences of his own children passing through different periods of experience.

Acolytes of either Piaget or Vygotsky blanch at media created for infants and toddlers because of how it seems to obliterate the distinctions between a six-month-old and a two-year-old. That is where much of the recent reconsideration of their theories is rooted. But in his eye-opening book *Anxious Parents: A History of Modern Childrearing in America,* social historian Peter N. Stearns offers a level-headed perspective. "The two major anxieties about children's entertainment developed at a somewhat different pace within the 20th century," he writes. "Concerns about monitoring the source and quality of children's toys and leisure activities go back into the late 19th century, as capitalist consumerism began to spread its tentacles to the American young. The idea of entertaining children as a responsibility, and particularly the power of the obligation to prevent boredom, surfaced gradually during the 1920s but emerged full force only in the 1940s and 1950s, when it became an integral part of what the sociologist Martha Wolfenstein perceptively dubbed the advent of a new fun morality." Over the last several decades, Stearns demonstrates, society has been convulsed at regular intervals with puritanical angst over the effect on kids of novels, silent movies, comic books, television, videogames, and the Internet.

Alarm bells over children being corrupted by media and popular culture have been ringing for decades, in other words. At the same time, though, it is worth noting that many of the reference points of recent history are, in the larger historical context, quite new. The word *boredom* became common only in the 19th century. The word *toddler* was invented by a department store mogul more recently than that.

But isn't the digitized, sped-up, while-u-wait 21st century fundamentally different from the horse-and-buggy 19th? Doesn't the array of electronic enticements for parents and kids make this a unique moment in the history of child development? I am writing this book in part to answer that question. I am not seeking to post a dire warning about the toxic effects of television on kids— itself a long-standing literary subgenre that includes such splenetic entries as *The Plug-In Drug* and *Endangered Minds*. These books are so strident that the pages are almost too stiff to turn, and they became bestsellers by playing to the paranoia of modern parents about the threats that lurk around every corner. Consider the dedication page of 1973 tract *Children's TV: The Economics of Exploitation,* which reads, "To Children, especially Sue Marie, Sandy, Chrissy and Jill."

Nor is *Anytime Playdate* intended as a corollary to Steven Johnson's *Everything Bad is Good for You,* to present a counterintuitive argument for the positive power of baby and preschool media. And despite the running references to my own family, it is not an addition to the burgeoning canon of navel-gazing parental memoirs.

This book is intended mainly as an examination of the boom's mechanics, the nexus of business, educational theory, and psychology at the heart of it. It is also a meditation on how television has defined two generations. Aside from being part of the first generation to have television at all, my father has worked in television almost since I was born. Having grown up not only as his product but as an acolyte of *Mister Rogers* and *Sesame Street,* I am now raising children in a dramatically more complex environment. One reason it is complex is that a "state of resonance" has replaced traditional communication, as Tony Schwartz, media theorist and Marshall McLuhan contemporary, memorably phrased it. "In communicating at electronic speed, we no longer direct information into an audience," he wrote, "but try to evoke stored information out of them, in a patterned way." Or, in the view of television critic Ron Powers, "Watching television . . . evokes a memory of television. Thus television becomes its own referent, its own test, its own standard for measuring validity."

In the pages to come, I will attempt to measure validity and evoke memories of raising children in television's third wave the best way I know how: by penetrating the secretive, sensitive process of making and marketing entertainment for babies and toddlers and also illuminating the struggle over entertainment's role in many households, including mine. I have gained access to the development of a preschool show on Nickelodeon's upcoming preschool schedule that is aiming to replicate *Dora the Explorer*'s cross-cultural success, only with a Chinese heroine. The core audience is a growing population of Asian viewers as well as upscale viewers increasingly bent on teaching their little corporate warriors-to-be Mandarin, the language of 21st-century business. Called *Ni Hao, Kai-lan* (Mandarin for "Hello, Kai-lan"), it was scheduled to debut in February 2008.

Like most preschool shows, *Ni Hao* is employing a "multiplatform strategy," the current buzz phrase for delivering content wherever kids are interested in seeing it. Gary Knell, CEO of Sesame Workshop, gave me an example from his stable that illustrates the modern imperatives. Sesame's planned revival of *The Electric Company* will debut in short episodes meant to be seen on a cell phone. It will then follow an increasingly common path, becoming a videogame, then a series of Web shorts, a DVD, and, finally, a TV show. This rollout is meant to address a pronounced, technology-driven shift in how children are guided through narrative stories. "People of a certain age, including many parents today, don't really regard it as 'technology,'" Knell said. "They just see it as stuff. Your daughter, for example, will not refer to a 'cell phone.' To her, it will just be 'the phone.'" I asked him if that meant that *The Electric Company,* originally intended for kids aged six, seven, and eight, would draw a lot of preschoolers, he noted that telecom companies are actively studying what is known in the trade as the "pass-back effect." That refers to what happens when preschoolers strapped into their car seats in the back clamor for adults in the front seat of a car to pass back their phones. Verizon Wireless carries "mobitoons" from Nickelodeon for just such a purpose. Sirius took note of that phenomenon in creating Backseat TV, a satellite service built into new cars by Chrysler, with programming from Nickelodeon and Disney. Knell pointed to the reality of "age compression," a trend that effectively makes the age threshold of most programs younger. *Sesame Street* has been one of the shows most vulnerable to age compression: its core viewers over the past decade have drifted downward from around four years old to two and a half.

The intersection of our household and the preschool industry revealed itself to me when a leaflet fell out of my daughter's *Barney* DVD case.

"You're invited to an Anytime Playdate!" it announced in a promotion for PBS Kids Sprout. The digital cable network, which launched in 2005, describes itself as "a preschool network where you'll find your favorite friends 24 hours a day." The leaflet is laid out to resemble a party invitation, with the following heading:

Where: Your TV

When: Whenever You Want

Who's coming: Barney & Friends, Bob the Builder, Angelina Ballerina, Thomas & Friends and more.

I started to wonder about all of Margot's playdates. She had formed attachments, learned lessons, and was sharing a meaningful portion of her life with characters I knew next to nothing about. DVDs and the DVR helped tide her over between live visits. I soon felt like a stereotypical parent, the kind I never envisioned becoming, worrying about my daughter as though she had just gone to the senior prom on the arm of a suspicious date. The leaflet also crystallized for me how the industry craftily manipulates an audience that could hardly be more vulnerable: kids under five and parents besieged by parenthood's many challenges. By adopting the role of friend or teacher, companies fend off criticism and gain trust. Noggin's official slogan is "It's like preschool on TV," and the network precedes episodes by explaining their many developmental benefits, in much the same way that sugary breakfast cereals used to advertise being "part of a nutritious breakfast." *Wonder Pets!,* one of Noggin's newly minted hits, "promotes phonological awareness," the channel asserts.

(Oh, well, in *that* case . . .) It's a recipe for dependency. "Everything is fine as long as the dosage is right," says an executive who works with preschool video brands such as *Teletubbies*. "It's prescription drugs being given without a prescription. If you take too much, you get a stomachache. If you take the right amount, your headache is gone."

As they calibrate the dosage, executives and creators of preschool programs also comport themselves in the manner of Hollywood rivals—typical for combatants on a multibillion-dollar business battlefield, but jarring given the age of their audience. "*Curious Buddies* is completely dead; they could never figure out how to sell it," an executive at Sesame Workshop dished to me about a line of Nickelodeon videos aimed at babies. A Nickelodeon executive shot darts at the Cartoon Network's preschool shows, promoted under the banner Tickle U, which debuted last fall. "It's a disaster in the ratings," she sneered. "How utterly stupid do you have to be to take the brand known for Adult Swim— all these racy cartoons at night—and try to do preschool? There's no way people are buying that."

This area of American culture and business is tracing the same boom trajectory that videogames did in the 1990s or that television itself did in the 1950s. From a societal standpoint, preschool media is at a more perilous juncture—not unlike where the auto industry was before SUV safety became a public relations issue or where Big Tobacco was before the legal sieges of the 1990s. It's a business growing explosively despite serious questions about the effects of its products and its aggressive marketing tactics, which for most companies begin with direct mail to pregnant mothers. Only two legitimate, comprehensive studies of baby and preschool media consumption have ever been completed, in 2003 and 2006 by the Kaiser Family Foundation, a private, nonprofit group dedicated to analyzing major health-care issues. Congressional calls to fund more research are stalled in committee, and there is a growing sentiment that it will be left to programmers and networks themselves to fund research, as pharmaceutical companies do with clinical drug trials.

The cone of ignorance that surrounds preschool entertainment results in some startling disconnects. Most producers of preschool content shrug at or openly ridicule the American Academy of Pediatrics' recommendation that no child under two be exposed to TV, and the Kaiser study found that just 6 percent of parents had ever heard of it. "Parents are blowing through that recommendation, whether it is out there or not," Knell said. "Who is to say that a twenty-two-month-old may not gain something educational from a program that's billed for her?" That twenty-two-month-old is what sets today's environment apart from that of previous decades, even though parents have always expressed uneasiness about the commercial bent or violent streak of what their children watch on TV. Today's households offer exponentially more ways for programmers to reach kids, and the default assumption is that families are open to those messages virtually from the time the children arrive home from the hospital. In some cases, it starts immediately postpartum; BabyFirstTV is negotiating with several hospitals in order to have its programming beamed into rooms where mothers and babies recover from delivery.

Entertainment companies often feel that the best defense against corruption charges is a good offense. They retain child psychology experts who maintain that, far from being harmful, these products are actually essential ways to help kids learn, just as I convinced myself on the morning that Margot first saw *Sesame Street*. Today's time-pressed, goal-oriented parents are certainly susceptible to that spin. "Parents seem to be allowing it in the household, maybe pushing it in the household," Knell said. "It's part of the generation of parents who grew up on *Sesame Street* and other shows who don't have the same kind of barriers that their parents had about the educational uses of television." Moreover, they are driven to achieve vicarious success, not just when their kids start applying to colleges but practically from the moment of conception. "A lot of our society is accelerating children faster than they need to be accelerated," said Dan Gurlitz, vice president of video at Koch Entertainment, which handles brands such as Brainy Baby and Baby Genius. "These products may *or may not* result in accelerated learning."

I hear that commonsense caveat everywhere. Even Sascha Paladino, head writer of *Ni Hao, Kai-lan*, told me, "I don't think kids under two should even be watching TV. The TV as babysitter is really a problem. So I don't think there's any way we can go about creating this show with the under two-year-old in mind." Alice Wilder, a longtime researcher at Nickelodeon, said, "I have told people here I am not comfortable working on audiences under two" Still, despite the honorable principles of people creating these programs, financial motives prevail. The jury is still out regarding the effects on the audience, but the factories keep churning out profitable product on the assumption that it makes our kids smarter. They're letting the marketplace decide. "If parents find that something is inappropriate, they won't buy it," an ex-Nickelodeon executive told me. "But even with all this fear and anxiety, one thing remains clear: more and more parents are putting their kids in front of the television." What's at stake is clear. The outcome of this conflicted period will determine nothing less than the nature of the next generation: how kids learn, interact, and come of age. And the consequences will radiate out across American society.

My intention, in *Anytime Playdate,* is to explore exactly how content gets to the screen, something that has seldom, if ever, been examined. Consumers and parents have a right to know how multibillion-dollar empires are built on the whims of two-year-olds, and how American culture arrived at this odd juncture where media conglomerates effectively hang on toddlers' every syllable.

Before my daughter was born, I did not often dwell on how quickly the world would want her to grow up. That reality hit me full force when she was almost two, during a family shopping outing to Century 21, a giant discount store in lower Manhattan across from the World Trade Center site. The store, essentially a grand-scale rival to Ross, Loehmann's, or TJ Maxx, stocks some well-known brands and some obscure ones, but the quality level is consistently high. If you don't mind the crowds and a fair amount of disarray in the grimy-carpeted aisles, it's a great place to pick up a Hugo Boss sport coat or pair of Cole Haan shoes for a fraction of their original price.

Clothing for Margot, a consistent need during her weed-like growth as a toddler, was the main reason for our trip. Who, I thought as we entered the store, wants to jam the mall and reflexively buy the same Baby Gap ensemble that every other American family is buying? Why not, for the same price, pick up something a little more offbeat? This, of course, is the mantra of the $1,100

Bugaboo stroller pushers, the parents who want a less assembly-line childhood for their kids. Public radio station KCRW in Santa Monica, California, has an on-air slogan that always makes me shake my head: "hand-picked music." The idea is to conjure a DJ combing through shelves of vinyl, compiling a completely original play list every day. The reality, of course, is quite different: a slick package of the latest offerings from well-known labels promoting a predetermined list of artists. But the "hand-picked" marketing has helped make KCRW a national powerhouse in music circles because what sells today is that which is "hand-picked," whether it's organic food or a customized entertainment experience.

Flipping through the racks at Century 21, I noticed something amazing: a vast selection of high-toned brands redirected to babies and toddlers: Armani Junior, Versace Young, Agnès B. Enfant, Sonia Rykiel Enfant, Lily Pulitzer, Moschino, Juicy Couture, and many more. A Juicy shirt for girls, available as small as size two, carried the capital-letter message (in case the point had eluded anyone) "Buy Me Stuff."

Clothing manufacturers have discovered what language tutors, ballet schools, and entertainment purveyors already knew: Generation X wants the best for their kids. That notion is centuries old, but my generation has put it in italics. We want the best in every sense, but especially in the material one. It would not do for kids to speak a single language or wear pants with iron-on patches. They should learn, speak, dress, and veg out on the couch just like their parents. This was the democratic new order of parenthood. Kids would come out of the womb bursting with potential, but, as optimistic as this view is on the one hand, it also leaves a yawning gap for exploitation on the other.

Tapping into a classic parental anxiety about nutrition, a New York entrepreneur has cannily developed a gourmet grocery store aimed at kids, called Kidfresh. Children push miniature carts around the scaled-down aisles, picking up tubs of hummus and baby carrots, or perhaps a packaged lunch with organic fruit salad, non-growth-hormone yogurt, and free-range turkey breast. As much as the store might "hand-pick" these ingredients for kids, the whole place is obviously geared toward parents, who are the ones footing the considerable bill. The feat of modern capitalism is making it appear as if it's all about the kids. For example, events called Baby Loves Disco, now held in twenty-one cities across the country, are full-scale disco dance parties for parents and babies, held in actual clubs with strobe lights and the usual trappings, only in the midday hours and with juice boxes replacing alcohol and drugs. The name says it all. Baby may not know what disco is, but he "loves" it mostly because Mommy and Daddy love the idea that they can still go out to a club.

To be honest, I must sheepishly recall a similar event my wife and I took part in, a rally organized by good friends when we lived in California. It was the spring of 2004 and the presidential election was just starting to heat up. Our friends, who were part of a baby group that we belonged to, staged a rally and designed T-shirts for all the kids that read "Babies Against Bush." We gathered on the streets of Santa Monica, a city known as the Berkeley of Southern California, and started marching around a three-block area, through an outdoor shopping mall, down to the ocean, and back again. "Babies Against Bush!" we all yelled. Cars honked in support. I felt uncomfortable then, and only agreed to wear the T-shirt and chant the chant because I truly did oppose Bush. Still, how do we know all the babies did, too? How would we know if they love disco? It's the power of projection inflated by the power of disposable income.

As child psychologist Bruno Bettelheim wrote in *The Uses*

of Enchantment, his still vital positioning of literary fairy tales designed for children, "Unfortunately, too many parents want their children's minds to function as their own do—as if mature understandings of ourselves and the world, and our ideas about the meaning of life, do not have to develop as slowly as our bodies and minds."

And so it is with the vast majority of entertainment for babies and toddlers. The presumption built into all of it is that it will make your child smarter, worldlier, better at science, better-spoken when he grows older. That was precisely where my journey began, on the floor with my daughter and Big Bird and the newspaper and my sacred cup of coffee. As much as I wanted to hold on to that pleasant memory, joined with my own distant childhood and my parents' recollections of the wonder of that glowing box in the living room, there were suddenly plenty of reasons to doubt what I was choosing to do.

At a conference I attended on children and media, Stanford professor Thomas Robinson upended many of my assumptions. "There is no evidence that co-viewing works," he said, pausing in the silence that followed to let his stem pronouncement sink in. "There's not even a lot of evidence that families actually *watch* together, even if they say they do. If they do watch, they're staring at the screen, not interacting with each other. If parents watch with their kids, the kids watch less kids' TV" and instead see less appropriate content. Rosemarie Truglio, who designed *Sesame Beginnings* as a proponent of co-viewing, conceded that fifteen consecutive minutes of watching together is all she could ever expect.

"The thing that amazes me," Robinson added, "is that these companies never talk about proof. Everyone running media companies is data-driven. They don't get up in the morning without looking at market research. And yet they get up here and say, 'We think this is a good show. I'd like my grandkids to see it.' Well, how about proving it?"

I decided to demand proof from even the fixtures of my world I had long taken for granted, characters and concepts that I had internalized decades before. Instead of what Schwartz had described as a "state of resonance," I wanted television to make sense somehow, to be a more rational, controllable force.

Being sensitized anew to the layers of meaning in the everyday would not be easy, however. Out for a run in Central Park, I looked across the expanse of green and realized it was the exact corner of the park where Big Bird leads a line of children in the opening title sequence to *Sesame Street*. A song came on my iPod that I had not listened to for a long while, "Toys" by XTC. I had always sung along, but never since my kids were born. The lyrics resonated in a new way as they cleverly describe how children so readily imitate their parents. I thought of Margot on the living room floor, seeing Big Bird for the first time, and how happy and proud that had made me. Were parents like me rushing children through the most important stage of development by dressing them up in Armani Junior and activating these endless electronic playdates, or were we just pawns in a new multibillion-dollar game? Journeying inside the machine was the only way to find out. As a child, I had adored *Mister Rogers' Neighborhood,* whose every episode featured a trolley traveling from Rogers's living room to the Land of Make Believe. The trolley was a device designed to help young viewers understand the relationship between the real world and the realm populated by puppet princesses. As an adult trying to understand the reality behind this digitized make-believe world, I would have to ride the same trolley in reverse. The Land of Make Believe would never look quite the same again.

2

FINDING *NI HAO*

Nickelodeon Plants the First Seeds

Karen Chau grew up watching TV on the sly. "I always had to sneak it on my dad's black-and-white set in the bathroom," she remembered. "But I *lived* for *The Cosby Show*. And I would go around humming *Smurfs* songs, not an easy thing to do in a Chinese household where it's all about classical piano."

From those early, surreptitious moments, Chau had a pretty good sense that she wouldn't be following in her father's footsteps. After leaving communist China with empty pockets in the early 1960s, Jack Chau found his way to Orange County in Southern California, where he became the multimillionaire owner of a seafood processing business. In the tradition of many recent immigrant populations, he urged his daughter to enter the business world or take a similar route to a presumably stable life.

Instead, Karen Chau did what any self-respecting digital art major would do upon graduating college (University of California at Irvine, in her case). She created a blog.

Her Web site became a repository for what Chau calls her "doodles and drawings," many of them inspired by her Chinese-American upbringing. At that point, her sole career goal was to become a children's book illustrator. But, as Web links often do, the blog found its way through friends who knew friends to a former Nickelodeon executive named Mary Harrington. Having shepherded Nick shows from *Rugrats* to *Ren & Stimpy,* Harrington had left the network nearly a decade earlier to become an independent producer. She was on the prowl for material that was visually appealing and had distinctive characters and personality. Enter Karen Chau and her alter ego, a five-year-old girl named Kai-lan. "A lot of her site wasn't really for me, but the stories about Kai-lan really spoke to me," Harrington said. "I usually develop things from drawings more than writing, and the artwork was really stunning." Looking at the illustrations for the first time, Harrington said her initial reaction was, "This is fantastic. I've hit the jackpot. Not only are these great designs, great little characters, but also we are tapping into Chinese culture and it is not manufactured."

Chau's style is influenced by animator Hayao Miyazaki and Yuko Shimizu, the creator of the Hello Kitty character. Kai-lan was surrounded by a fantastical world of animals, vivid flowers, and a smiling sun. Everything, from dumplings to clouds to flowers, had facial features. Kai-lan palled around with her grandfather and a host of animal friends, including a small bear and a pink rhino suspended by a balloon. Early drawings Chau made on Adobe Illustrator burst with color and wit. In one, a shirtless Kai-lan pushes a cart through a supermarket produce aisle, stopping by a pyramid of anthropomorphic pineapples.

After meeting with Chau in 2003 and seeing more of her artwork, Harrington decided to develop the material into a potential series. The usual process in preschool, as in much of TV development, is for a pilot to be ordered and then a series based on the progress of the pilot. Harrington showed Chau's work to Brown Johnson, head of Nickelodeon Preschool, hoping to receive a series order. Johnson immediately sparked to the characters but opted to have Harrington and Chau produce three two-minute shorts, to be budgeted under a program called My World designed to expand Nickelodeon's contact with show creators from diverse ethnic backgrounds. The shorts would air first online, and then on Nick Jr. and Noggin.

Executives told Harrington the shorts fit perfectly with the idea they had of doing a show with a social-emotional curriculum. *Sesame Street* had dealt with emotions, as had *Mister Rogers* and *Barney*. But in the 21st-century preschool world, entire shows built expressly around emotion were still rare because they are not easy to pull off. "It's hard for young children to notice emotions," said Laura G. Brown, a consultant who wound up working extensively with Harrington and Chau. "Kai-lan is able to make the point that it's worth it for them to stop the tape and roll it back and think about why we feel the way they feel."

Suddenly, the doodles and drawings were on their way to becoming a full-blown trio of animated shorts, which presented a dilemma. How would the shorts retain the spirit of the Web site and what story could be created for them to tell?

"We naively proceeded," Harrington said. "We didn't know exactly what direction it would take as far as the curriculum. We wanted to develop it for what we thought would be good for a television show.

"I'm not a schoolteacher and neither is Karen. We didn't go

down the road of doing what we're not comfortable with, like saying, 'We'll be a math show' or 'We'll be *this* kind of show.' We just wanted to bring this girl to life."

They wound up producing the three short episodes under the title *Downward Doghouse:* "Follow That Slipper," "Where's HoHo?" and "Dragon Dance." In each, Kai-lan addresses the viewer and begins "Ni-Hao, ma. That means, 'How are you?'" She then walks over to the sun and offers her daily greeting: "Hello, sun in the sky, sitting oh so very high / Up we go, down we go, stretching out to say hello." Each of the three shorts has a plot that is easy to summarize: a grasshopper crawls inside a slipper and hops away; a monkey named HoHo hides in the bushes; on Dragon Day, everyone does a special dance.

The show's original name, *Downward Doghouse,* reflected the plan to present a "yoga-related coping mechanism" in conjunction with the emotional curriculum, according to Brown. "Originally, we were going to explore the mind-body connection," Chau said. "I thought, 'Oooh, we're going to do some kangaroo hops and "stretch your neck like a giraffe."'" Brown describes the educational goal of one early script as "teaching how to use your body to help deal with anger." Kay Wilson Stallings, the Nickelodeon executive who shepherded the series, said the focus on yoga was a reaction to ubiquitous media reports about childhood obesity. "Then when we picked up *LazyTown,*" a live-action series in which Sportacus, the hero, battles Robbie Rotten with an emphasis on fitness and nutrition, "we decided that was a more organic way to have a fitness component, so we said, 'Let's pull back on the yoga and focus on emotional intelligence.'"

Chau's aesthetic was well in evidence even at this early stage: exaggerated, oversize oval heads, grass the bright color of tree frogs, bushes rustling, lily pads floating. The pace was brisk but not frenetic, the cross-cultural aspects clear but not over the top. The shorts drew steady traffic online and made a positive impression on the air based on viewer feedback. As it contemplated the fate of the shorts, the network ran tests in March 2005, polling parents online and conducting live focus groups in Manhattan. "The response we got across the board was that the kids thought the shorts were too short," Wilson Stallings said. "They wanted more." As they explored the potential to expand on the shorts, in the summer of 2005, Nickelodeon launched them online and soon thereafter they entered the rotation on Nick Jr. and Noggin.

Brown Johnson, president of Nickelodeon Preschool, saw something worth a gamble. Having studied visual art at Hampshire College, the experimental school that opened in 1970 as an alternative to neighboring Smith, Amherst, Mount Holyoke, and the University of Massachusetts, she was impressed by the aesthetic of *Downward Doghouse,* which was unlike that of any other Nickelodeon preschool offerings. In her nearly two decades as the company's preschool guru, Johnson had often demonstrated a gift for aesthetics, scrutinizing the color palette, texture, and animation style of every show and building a portfolio of preschool offerings that featured no two shows alike. Also in *Doghouse*'s favor, the Beijing Olympics were set for the summer of 2008, and trends in the business world and society pointed to Mandarin and Chinese culture being essential features of the 21st-century landscape. In bigger U.S. cities, Mandarin-speaking nannies and language tutors command top dollar from achievement-oriented parents hoping to raise the perfect little corporate warrior. Under Johnson's leadership, Nickelodeon had also reaped billions from another animated bilingual heroine,

Those factors, plus the positive test scores,
ial order in October 2005 of twenty 22-min-
n Chau's "doodles" were about to become an
ies.

In 2003, when *Downward Doghouse* first went into development, Nickelodeon occupied a position in popular culture and the
preschool business that was dominant to an extent unimaginable
during the long public-broadcasting reign of *Sesame Street* and
Mister Rogers' Neighborhood. Of the top ten programs on cable
TV intended for the two-to-five demographic group, Nickelodeon
aired nine of them. In overall ratings, it held a wide lead over any
other kids channel and had consistently been one of the top-rated
networks in all of cable. It is striking, in retrospect, to realize that
the planets were aligning to allow for Nickelodeon to launch in
the 1970s at the very same time PBS and Children's Television
Workshop, the producer of *Sesame Street* (and now called Sesame
Workshop), were staking their claim as children's TV leaders.
Nickelodeon's first flagship program, *Pinwheel,* closely resembled
Sesame Street in many respects.

The first head of Nickelodeon was Cy Schneider, a veteran of
ad giant Ogilvy & Mather who had engineered campaigns for
several children's brands, notably Barbie and Hot Wheels. His
hiring resulted from a request from his ad clients to consult with
Warner Communications, the company that eventually morphed
into what is now Time Warner. Company executives told Schneider they wanted to start a cable network for kids—what they
called "a bright and shining new light for children's television."

The commercial-free channel would aim to provide an alternative to commercial broadcast fare, which parents for years had been increasingly protesting due to concerns about violence or blatant merchandising.

The cornerstone show of early Nickelodeon was also the channel's name for its first four years: *Pinwheel*. The hourlong program drew from sources that remain at the core of Nickelodeon's DNA: the consumer marketplace and interactive technology. Warner Amex, a fifty-fifty venture of Warner Communications and American Express, funded Nickelodeon's launch on April 1, 1979. Its programs were largely derived from an earlier channel on a service called QUBE, which was even fringier than cable, and was thought to have potential as a home-shopping outlet that would entice people to use their American Express cards. The thirty-channel experiment in interactive television began in 1977 in Columbus, Ohio. It had a remote control with eighteen buttons, movies for purchase at three dollars per viewing and a set-top box premium-priced at two hundred dollars that featured a dial-up modem. Way ahead of its time, especially coming a full generation before the Internet, the system would lose about $30 million before Warner eventually bought out American Express and took full control. Two QUBE channels would go on to change global pop culture and generate untold billions: Sight on Sound, which would evolve into MTV, and Pinwheel, which became Nickelodeon.

Borrowing the puppetry that was a historical kids-TV staple and adding the animated flair that became Nickelodeon's trademark, *Pinwheel* episodes featured actors interacting with puppets, interspersed with animated segments. The main action took place at Pinwheel Playhouse, which was located, according to creator Craig Marin, "on the back roads of your memory in the

29

magical corner of the Imagine Nation." The theme song, against an impressionistic animated title sequence showing life in an imaginary town, struck an appealingly simple chord: "Pinwheel, pinwheel, spinning around / look at my pinwheel and see what I've found." Staple characters included Smitty (editor of the *Daily Noodle* newspaper), ambiguous duo Plus and Minus, Molly O'Mole, Silas the Snail, a pair of "hobo bugs" named Herbert and Lulu, and Coco the mime.

However warmly *Pinwheel* was received, it didn't prove to be the foundation of a network strategy that would separate Nick from PBS. It helped Nickelodeon win a Peabody Award in 1982. That would have been a treasured milestone for a three-year-old nonprofit, but for a startup cable network that was very much *for*-profit, it was not a measure of kids' undying loyalty and the dollars that usually flow from that. Some blamed the stewardship of founding chief Cy Schneider, pointing out that his knack for selling toys to kids in the three-network era differed starkly from creating a commercial answer to PBS in the dawning cable age.

At that point, the broadcast networks generally hadn't lost sleep thinking about how to brand themselves, aside from jockeying over news, sports, and the occasional prime-time star. Their audience was remarkably steady between the early 1950s and the late 1970s, and the government's consideration of them as quasi-public utilities kept the noise of promotion to a dull roar. But cable outlets, competing for targeted ad dollars and niche audiences, had to set themselves apart through aggressive and canny marketing, not just sheer spending. (That imperative remains today, as witnessed by Cartoon Network's disastrous "street-team" stunt to plug its series *Aqua Teen Hunger Force*, which resulted in a national-security shutdown of the city of Boston in January 2007. Passersby mistook an electronically illuminated device beaming images from the show for a bomb. It cost the network $2 million in a settlement with residents and businesses affected and the swift hara-kari exit of the network's chief.)

Before becoming first head of Nickelodeon, Schneider had already blazed some trails. As an adman with Mattel, he co-wrote a commercial in 1955 for the Burp Gun that is remembered as the first toy commercial ever aired. Over the next generation, he worked to meld the worlds of Madison Avenue and children's programming, helping ABC repackage old Baby Huey cartoons into a show hosted by the synergistically named Mattey Mattel. He also launched the show *Hot Wheels,* which took the sponsor-programmer relationship, which had been cozy since the late 1940s, all the way to full-time promotion. *Hot Wheels* was cited by Action for Children's Television, the potent activist group founded by four suburban Boston housewives in the late 1960s, as one of the chief culprits in the overly commercialized landscape of kids TV. "Television has become an intrinsic part of most children's experience," ACT founders Peggy Charren and Lillian Ambrosino wrote in 1968. "Children's television can be changed!"

Schneider "believed in an advertising approach that said to kids in a booming voice, 'This is fun! Come watch us!'" recalled Geraldine Laybourne, a former schoolteacher, researcher, and independent producer who got to Nickelodeon in 1980. Hired along with Schneider in 1980, she worked for him until his departure in 1984 and now runs the cable network Oxygen. "The kids heard a male voice saying, 'Come watch us' and tuned it in but it wasn't fun and it was 'good-for-you green vegetables' so they felt betrayed by the 'this is fun!' Yes, we got off to a rocky start." Schneider, Laybourne believed, "came to it with a guilty conscience but I came to it with a pure heart. He made us do things that were so awful for kids. They were so earnest. . . . [Corporate boss] Bob

Pittman used to joke, 'We needed to bring in a schoolmarm to take the schoolmarm out of the network.'"

The lack of commercials, the Peabody, the wholesome, PBS-ness of *Pinwheel* . . . it did all seem an odd fit for Schneider. Later, in his memoir *Children's Television: The Art, the Business, and How it Works,* he made some stark pronouncements that few in today's preschool industry would echo publicly. Children's TV, he wrote, "is a business that makes money by selling products. Television's first mission is not to inform, educate or enlighten. It isn't even to entertain. Its first mission is to entice viewers to watch the commercials." Looking back at the launch of the network, he added, "I wish I could say with some degree of honesty that it was Warner-Amex's or my own genuine desire to provide better, more inspiring children's programming because of a burning sense of social responsibility. I can't . . . Nickelodeon, for all its lofty aims and subsequent broadcasting awards, was and is a product born of the demands of the marketplace."

Even under such seemingly conflicted leadership, Nickelodeon couldn't help but grow along with the rest of cable, whose ad revenue soared from $58 million in 1980 to $546 million in 1984, as the number of channels nearly tripled to twenty-three in 1985. But it would not vault to the front ranks and mark the broader culture with bright orange footprints until 1984, when Laybourne began a rise that would see her eventually run the whole network. She helped transform a shrewd but still underappreciated idea—a twenty-four-hour channel with parent-approved kids content—into an object of obsession for anyone under twelve years of age. "My son, Sam, wore a Nickelodeon hat to camp when he was five," Laybourne recalled. "He came home sobbing and threw it in the closet. I thought somebody had bullied him but he told me that the kids had made fun of the hat. They called it a doody channel. I decided right then that we were going to have to correct this impression."

There was another crucial reason for Nickelodeon's blossoming in the 1980s: against a backdrop of shows from *Strawberry Shortcake* to the *Care Bears* selling all manner of tie-in products and winning consumer loyalty based on single characters or series, Nickelodeon succeeded in branding itself as a network. That is the norm today—consider current examples such as Comedy Central, ESPN, or HBO—but at the time it was revolutionary. With its Day-Glo orange logo and exuberant celebration of all things kids, Nickelodeon possessed the same bravura shot of energy that transformed MTV into a cultural force. Not coincidentally, liftoff for both was achieved after they were sold to Viacom, still their parent company, for $700 million in 1985.

Preschool was not Laybourne's immediate mandate, however, so she delivered energy in other areas first. By reinvesting revenues from the Viacom buyout and early hits like *Double Dare* into original animation, the share of the day's schedule devoted to animation increased from 3.5 hours in 1985 to 15.5 hours a decade later. Most of her energy went into programs for grade-schoolers, among them *You Can't Do That on Television, Double Dare, Rugrats*, and *Ren & Stimpy*, as well as an adult initiative, Nick at Nite, that played old sitcoms when kids were presumed to be in bed. (The latter concept succeeded to the point that it led to the launch of the TV Land channel.) Still, Laybourne and her colleagues recognized that the Reagan era's deregulation wave had ushered in an absurd number of syndicated kids shows, many pandering to the preschool age group, that were barely disguised product plugs for G.I. Joe, He-Man, and the like. The number of shows based on toys, many of them funded by toymakers themselves, soared from thirteen in 1980 to more than seventy in 1987. The Federal Communications Commission, in a 1985 report, declared these shows "in the public interest" and refused to limit them.

On the other end of the spectrum were *Sesame Street* and *Mister Rogers,* which still remained the gold standard but had evolved little. Nickelodeon saw an opportunity to balance quality and commerce for the 2–5 demo, and came up with the preschool division known as Nick Jr. The subset would also help the mother ship guard against the damage that could result from grade-schoolers reacting to "Big Nick" as Laybourne's own son had initially, by considering it a "baby channel." The year was 1988, two years before Congress would approve the Children's Television Act requiring broadcasters (but not cable networks) to air a certain amount of educational or informational programming. The act was reinforced in 1996 with a specific threshold of six hours of such programming. Nick Jr. officially launched as a programming block in 1993.

The '80s were marked by much more than deregulation. It was also an era of social ills affecting children in more direct and unprecedented ways. "It was the first time that kids were dealing with parents getting divorced and then going back to the workforce. This was the first generation that had to deal with confidant problems," Laybourne said. "Their mothers were asking them questions that were totally inappropriate for kids. The parents were very self-involved and kids were dealing with issues way over their heads." One of the guiding texts for those formative times, Laybourne said, was Tufts child development expert David Elkind's *Hurried Child,* a 1981 book about parental pressure on kids that remains in print and remains relevant even twenty-six years later.

"In 1984, we did research in Danbury, Connecticut, four groups of ten-year-old kids," Laybourne recalled. "It was horrifying. They were telling us, 'We're being pressured to grow up. Our brains are shrinking.' They'd heard about teen pregnancy and teen suicide and I was like, 'Whoa. These kids need a place for childhood.' And that was the lightbulb. We said, 'OK, we're going to be a place that has their sense of humor, that's on their side, where they can just be kids.'"

While broadcasters and PBS—whose budget was strafed by years of Republican-majority fire in Washington—were both bullied and shamed by the government about their efforts to engage kids, Nickelodeon saw a huge moneymaking opportunity in planting seeds with kids as young as two. "We recognize that if we start getting kids to watch us at this age, we have them for life," Laybourne said about Nick Jr. "That's exactly why we were doing it." PBS had also started racking up staggering merchandise sales from *Barney,* a show that altered the landscape radically upon its debut in 1992. "We saw what happened with *Barney;* those very simple love messages, irritating as they are to adults, did something right, which was speak directly to kids," said Laybourne. "We had some beautiful shows and then we saw with *Barney* how simple is beautiful. We thought, 'We can't be so elaborate.'" Alice Cahn, the preschool chief at Cartoon Network who was at PBS during the 1990s, describes it this way: "It really wasn't until the juggernaut of *Barney* that people said, 'two hundred thousand dollars for a half hour, four hundred licensees in three years; OK, it's a business!'"

Once the mission of aiming straight at kids was articulated, both internally and to viewers, Nickelodeon started growing exponentially, both in financial terms and as the top-rated producer of preschool programming. Under Herb Scannell, who succeeded Laybourne in 1996, the network launched *Blue's Clues* and *Dora the Explorer* and created Noggin, the channel that began as a partnership with Sesame Workshop. "More and more, Nick is like CNN for children," Nintendo vice president George Harrison, speaking for many ad buyers, told the *Philadelphia Inquirer* in 1998. "It's just the thing they turn to." When Viacom merged with CBS in 2000, a popular aphorism began to circulate in media circles and on Wall Street, eventually being repeated by executives themselves: Viacom was now able to provide "cradle to the grave" television service. It could wean customers on Noggin, transition them to Nick, upsell them to MTV, then VH1, then CBS, and finally, in the autumn of their years, to the comforting black-and-white laugh tracks on Nick at Nite.

Only in recent years has Nickelodeon started to appear somewhat vulnerable, due mainly to increased competition in a market it essentially created. After a run of more than a decade as the dominant player, Nick found itself under assault from Disney, which had extended the *Baby Einstein* series of infant videos to the preschool series *Little Einsteins*. Disney's *High School Musical* went off like a nuclear charge in 2006, earning astronomical Nielsen ratings. More important, it created an entire new universe of new stars—a movie called *Jump In!* starring Corbin Bleu from *High School Musical*, rated even higher than the mega-hit original, and Disney has mobilized an array of sequels and spin-offs. High School Musical 2 in August 2007 was the most-watched program in cable TV history. The third installment will be a theatrical feature. Licensing opportunities, from soundtracks to stage shows, abound. "It isn't like we were number one and then, suddenly, we were number two," notes a Nickelodeon marketing staffer. "But everybody got incredibly anxious once they realized they were facing strong competition for the first time in a long time." Officially, the network waves away questions about Disney, insisting that because the Disney Channel is commercial-free, that it isn't a true competitor. But the gamesmanship continued apace as 2007 drew to a close. When Nickelodeon would schedule a show, Disney would counter-program with a rerun of a popular show aimed at a similar audience, so that it could dent Nickelodeon even if it didn't win the time period in terms of ratings. Scheduling was a cloak-and-dagger affair, with Disney waiting until days before airtime to announce its lineup in an effort to mount effective stealth attacks.

Scannell departed in 2005 amid speculation among the Nickelodeon rank and file that it was not entirely voluntary, and was replaced by Cyma Zarghami, whose purview included far more than just Nickelodeon. Her title is head of MTV Family. The change ushered in something of a cultural sea change for Nickelodeon. Scannell, who had fostered many hit franchises, utilized an avuncular and encouraging management style. "We would get e-mails on Friday mornings congratulating us for a big premiere and giving us the afternoon off," recalls one staffer. "With Cyma, the job is more demanding and you feel like she's always waiting for results." Another veteran executive says, "For Cyma, it's all about winning. She's very focused and no-nonsense, but a lot of that is because of how big her domain is."

Amid the corporate reshuffling, the longtime steward of Nick's preschool efforts, Brown Johnson, got a promotion to the head of Nickelodeon Preschool. For longtime employees, it was a welcome sign that Zarghami largely gave Johnson a long leash. Johnson measures the duration of shows and her own longevity in terms of her seventeen-year-old daughter, who was born when Johnson was at Nickelodeon. She has seen an entire generation grow up on Nickelodeon programming and is largely revered internally as the "godmother of preschool TV." She shepherded *Blue's Clues* and *Dora the Explorer*—the twin billion-dollar drivers of Nickelodeon in the previous decade. Although clearly immersed in commerce, Johnson makes the impression of an enthusiastic student of everything around her. She has a penchant for uptalk, her phrases often rising into an implied question.

"The nice thing about Nick Jr. is that we started before there was pressure," Johnson says, sitting in one of the primary-colored conference rooms at Nickelodeon's Times Square headquarters in New York. "We could just fling things at the wall and see what stuck." *Blue's Clues* was a giant crapshoot. The show brought preschool television to new heights of both quality and commercial potency. Steeped in the research of Daniel Anderson of the University of Massachusetts, who had debunked the notion that children are passive viewers of television, *Blue's Clues* helped pioneer interactivity as a driver of educational content. Previous shows featured direct address to kids, but this one was built around kids helping the host find clues and solve puzzles. It was "scaffolded" such that viewers of ages two, three, four, and five would connect with it in different ways. The colors were vibrant and simple, and the computer-generated backgrounds surrounding the human host were kept minimal and easy to follow. It was a hit from the time it first aired in 1996. "Parents in focus groups said to us, 'I don't know, my kids are never going to watch that show,'" Johnson said, "but meanwhile in the next room kids were motionless waiting to help Steve."

Johnson's instinct for hits was not honed in an MBA program. She left college without a degree and went to New York, where she found a job working for Bauhaus architect Marcel Breuer, known for designing New York's Whitney Museum and tubular steel furniture such as the Wassily chair. Along with her artistic side, another part of her responded during that time she was immersed in the 1970s New York design world, perhaps the ultimate nexus of art and commerce. "Their process was interesting dealing with clients, having a really creative creator needing to fulfill work needs and people and flow of information," she said.

From Breuer she moved to *Mademoiselle* magazine. As merchandising editor, "I sold promotions to department stores and did makeovers on location. I used to travel with a makeup artist and a hairstylist. There would be two fashion editors and we would grab clothes." Looking back, she said it taught her about "thinking on my feet, planning ahead. I think it was that I spent a lot of time onstage talking to people. Who knows? It was all fairly random. . . . But it was the same idea about how media can influence a person and help them become who they are."

From there, she worked as an acquisitions executive for Vestron Video (best remembered for distributing *Dirty Dancing*). Soon she made a fateful connection, working as Bob Pittman's assistant. One of the architects of MTV and Nickelodeon by virtue of his early role at the QUBE channels, Pittman was running Showtime and Movie Channel at the time. "I was such a crappy assistant that he promoted me," Johnson said. "I put together the Movie Channel schedule before there were computers. I had an electric typewriter and I used to schedule with this giant plastic sheet that had lines for all the days of the month, thirty days, twenty-four hours of the day, different colors for different kinds of movies."

This pragmatic skill, mixed with an artist's taste, as well as her role as a mom, positioned Johnson to lead Nickelodeon into preschool. Unlike other bottom-line executives, including Zarghami, Johnson focused on seemingly minute details, such as whether the palette of a press kit matched that of the show it was promoting. She kept a large bouquet of shows in her head and knew how to match textures, colors, themes to create an arrangement that would sell.

"About seventeen years ago, before Nick Jr. got reinvented, we had a two-day meeting of people from all walks of life—storytellers, authors, elementary school principals, a producer from *Mister Rogers' Neighborhood*, psychologists, professors, poets, people who taught teachers how to teach," she said. "Two days of talking very idealistically about what entertainment could and should be for kids. What values it should have, even things like what the screen should look like."

As a mom, Johnson felt personally drawn to preschool fare. "I've also always been interested in the ways that media affects people, what lessons you learn, whether it's a page of a magazine or a television show, about how people treat each other, what's the right way to settle an argument. ('OK, pull out your gun. Mmmaybe not such a good choice.') So that was a long time ago and we made some great, fast friends. We met some toymakers there. Out of that came our whole idea that you can use TV to play to learn, too. So you can put a lot of learning into a very playful and engaging story and have it be even more meaningful because it is so engaging and you like the characters so much. It's the Mister Rogers philosophy. That's what Joe and Steve are on *Blue's Clues*."

At Nickelodeon, Johnson said she has often told her employees, "Everything's educational—good lessons or provocative or inspiring ones. You're going to learn something, whether it's that all girls are princesses or all boys want guns. But I think one of the differences for Nick Jr. and one of the things that we do well is creating a really good connection between the audience and the TV. It started with our host character called Face. It was just a big smiling face who would talk to you. When we launched Face, we were really nervous that we'd get letters from parents saying, 'Why is the television talking to my child? He's too weird. It's the ghost in the machine, bad, bad, bad.' But he was just funny. He wasn't telling them to mail him money or anything. And then Steve from *Blue's Clues* took that idea one step further. Kids at home really felt that Steve couldn't be successful unless they told him where the clue was. He never found the clues by himself. Kids used to write us saying, 'I really think Steve needs glasses, because the clues are right there.' So they're very earnest in their need to help him and truly believe that he is waiting for them. That was that long pause that no one had really done before on TV. We were playing around with making computer games for kids. In computer games, you have to wait for kids to comprehend what is on the screen."

Entertainment and education met halfway at Nickelodeon. That sentiment had been repeated to me many times by people who worked there. The network was not going to try to duplicate what Children's Television Workshop achieved, only to carry forward its best elements and then add a visual aesthetic that seemed newly possible in the cable-happy 1980s.

"It meant the screen had to be really simple," Johnson said. "How you read goes left to right, the most important character says the most important stuff. He or she always says something three times. We have a lot of rules for everything from how the characters stand out against the background to how many cuts there are in a show. *Blue's Clues* in the early episodes had about twelve cuts. What happens with a cut is that kids either turn away or they pay attention because they're so literal in their understanding of TV action."

In the spring of 2006, Johnson's next creation, *Downward Doghouse,* was revealed to the press and advertising executives at Nickelodeon's glitzy "up-front" presentation to media buyers. Each network stages fairly elaborate presentations a few months before (or "up front" of) the traditional September-through-May TV season. The show merited only a small clip during a longer reel promoting new and continuing series, but a press release that day got picked up on a range of animation and TV blogs, putting it on the media radar.

A press release announcing that the premiere was set for March 2007 said *Downward Doghouse* was developed and produced through a partnership between Nickelodeon and Wang Films. It was described as "a new, original animated series that introduces preschoolers to the many aspects of Chinese culture and language through a five-year-old Chinese-American girl named Kai-lan. Following in the tradition of *Dora the Explorer* and *Go, Diego, Go!,* this new play-along series features an intergenerational Chinese-American family and teaches the Mandarin language to preschoolers at home—a first for preschool television. Each half-hour centers on Kai-lan and her relationships with her grandfather, her animal friends, and the natural world. Kai-lan is an emotionally gifted child who is driven to understand the world and how things are linked together both physically and emotionally. Every episode follows the adventures of Kai-lan and her friends as they learn to identify their emotions and stop to consider the feelings of others. The series explores the colorful aspects of Kai-lan's upbringing and background including family, food, and language while encouraging preschoolers to care for others and their environment."

The organic nature of the show and its outgrowth from Chau's own personal experience were undeniable assets. There are sixty thousand Chinese children who have been adopted by U.S. parents (including Jade-Lianna Peters, who does the voice of Kai-lan). The hard part was going to be blending Chau's original creation with far loftier goals and to create inviting story lines.

Just as the hard work of *Downward Doghouse* was beginning, Nickelodeon launched *Go, Diego, Go!*, the spin-off from *Dora*, and saw it take off immediately. While it didn't explicitly teach bilingualism as Dora did, Diego was her cousin and the show's undefined tropical backdrop looked almost identical. There were other similarities. While Dora had Backpack, Diego had Rescue Pack; while Dora had a companion named Boots, Diego had his sister Alicia and Click the camera. *Downward Doghouse* would not be able to follow such a circumscribed path. It would require creating an entirely new setting, cast of characters, and value system. The show represented a wager of several million dollars on China becoming ever more in the zeitgeist in the years to come.

3

ATTENTIONAL INERTIA

Parsing Preschool TV Research

As she set about building Nickelodeon into a kids empire, Geraldine Laybourne recognized that one particular element had to be at its center. "As soon as I got there, I said, 'We are not putting anything on the air without research,'" she recalls. "Even though we didn't have a research budget, we put a television at the Children's Museum of New York. It was two blocks from our office. To me, it was infinitely better to have a couple of kids looking at stuff than to not have anything." From that initial impulse grew one of the entertainment world's most sophisticated research cultures, with series being tested hundreds of times and development concepts getting shaped by feedback from the audience. Over time, it became a key selling point. Judy McGrath, head of MTV Networks and for many years the uberboss of everyone at Nickelodeon, touted the network's "powerful, in-depth research" at a 2006 presentation to advertisers and proclaimed its "deep understanding of kids."

In some respects, that notion wasn't completely novel. Television programmers, along with consumer advertisers and political candidates, had been systematically trying to refine their messages for decades. What did set Nickelodeon apart, though, is the way it married academic research with conventional market research. The combination is personified by Dan Anderson, the University of Massachusetts psychology professor who is considered one of the deans of academic researchers looking at the effect of TV on kids under five. After beginning his career in the early 1970s convinced that TV viewing was a passive activity for preschool kids and with no intellectually stimulating qualities, he wound up proving in his lab that the opposite is often true.

As he proceeded in the next few years to establish in more detail how much kids were thinking as they watched, Anderson hit the radar screen of Laybourne and her executive team at Nickelodeon. They invited him in 1993 to serve as a consultant on the development of Nick Jr. shows, furthering the interplay between academia and the preschool industry. "Because Nickelodeon was interested in providing programs that would actually benefit preschools rather than merely entertain them, I jumped at the chance," Anderson later wrote. He soon connected with a young researcher named Angela Santomero, who had studied Anderson's work as a student in psychology and child development and wanted to channel some of its precepts into her own show. The show turned out to be *Blue's Clues,* and Anderson's role was pivotal, both as the initial inspiration for creating it and as the chief adviser shaping it as a result of kids' input. For a section of his book, *The Tipping Point*, Malcolm Gladwell spent time with Anderson and others involved with *Blue's Clues*. He positioned the show as representing a tip away from *Sesame Street* and toward an interactive, computer-generated, and narrative-driven future.

One of Anderson's many important findings with *Blue's Clues,* in addition to the fact that it improved certain regular viewers' cognitive abilities, was that it appealed to preschoolers by telling a straightforward story instead of the chopped-up "magazine" approach of *Sesame Street.* Before coming to Nickelodeon, he had identified something he and his colleagues called "attentional inertia," which he described as the "deepened engagement with television that begins when a viewer initiates a look at the TV, reaching a state of engagement after about 15 seconds of continuous looking that further deepens as the look continues." Infants as young as three months have displayed attentional inertia, which manifests itself physiologically with a decelerated heart rate (an indicator of focused attention), reduced distractibility, and sharper memory of what is on the screen. In short, attentional inertia allows learning to happen, and magazine shows such as *Sesame Street,* which traditionally showed up to forty segments an hour, were less effective at inducing attentional inertia than *Blue's Clues,* whose patented "pause" and simple, contained environment and linear story all worked in its favor.

Alice Wilder, a child development expert who was the head researcher for *Blue's Clues* and is now working on the PBS series *Super Why!* said the multiplying number of shows in the marketplace also brings a variety of approaches to research. The Disney Channel, for example, started in-house research from scratch when it created its preschool block, Playhouse Disney. Often, the chicken-and-egg balance between education and entertainment is evident in research. "Many shows are created by a person who has a story to tell or a show idea," Wilder said. "Then that person says to a consultant, 'Help me write a curriculum that overlays onto my show idea and make that curriculum work.' Then there are creators who say, 'I really want to teach kids *this,* and here is my creative vision for how to integrate that into a story.' That was the case with Angela Santomero and *Blue's Clues*. With the latter case, it's connecting the dots as you go. With the overlay, it's about 'We can call this that and fit this in here and here.'"

In the beginning, before Anderson's career and before cable TV, research on preschool TV took a single form: the CTW Model. Named for *Sesame Street* production company Children's Television Workshop (now called Sesame Workshop), it served as a template for children's TV research—specifically how it interacts with the creation of scripts, characters, and show concepts—that had not existed in the first two decades of the medium's history. That delayed realization of the care required to produce a show of the caliber of *Sesame Street* is in part a result of the fact that in America, unlike in most other countries, public television came after commercial television. In some ways, the CTW Model continues to define the preschool landscape, eliminating the walls that historically separated the writers and producers from the people examining the effect of a program. Mary Harrington, one of the producers of *Ni Hao, Kai-lan* who is a Nickelodeon veteran but new to the realm of preschool, told me during one of the show's first focus groups, "This is great for me because they never used to let executives anywhere near this process."

In an essay in *G is for Growing: Thirty Years of Research on Children and Sesame Street,* four of the show's researchers describe the CTW Model this way: "Since the inception of *Sesame Street,* the voice of the child has been incorporated continuously into the development of the show. The creators believed that the best way to develop and evaluate a quality educational television program was to consult with the true experts—preschool children—and get their reactions. From the beginning, the creators of *Sesame Street* designed this entertaining, educational show as an experimental research project that would bring together educational advisors, researchers and television producers as equal partners." After ideas are contributed by all these constituents, they are then tested and retested and tested some more before actual production—the most expensive phase of any show's existence—begins.

Sometimes, even after production is finished, fatal flaws are discovered during a final round of testing. Such was the case in 1992, when sociological data trends and plain common sense guided *Sesame Street* to attempt to tackle the subject of divorce, in an episode titled "Snuffy's Parents Get a Divorce." In testing the fully produced episode, in which the parents of Snuffy and Alice, two snuffleupaguses who live on Sesame Street, split up, CTW sampled the reactions of sixty preschoolers at four different day-care centers. That test followed a scrupulous review of every word of the script over a span of many months. An internal report on the final test revealed "several unintended negative effects." Kids could not grasp the assertion in the script that Snuffy and Alice's parents still loved each other despite the divorce. They were confused by references to where the father lived; many of them believed he had run away and that Snuffy and Alice "would never see him again." A solid majority believed that an argument between parents would lead to divorce, despite the adult character Gordon's level-headed assertion that it was not always the case. The result of that last-minute glitch? The episode never aired. The move carried a financial cost but the consensus was that the risk of negative impact on viewers was too great.

Virtually all the successful shows for preschoolers launched since *Sesame Street* can trace their roots directly to the CTW Model, as people involved with the show have gone on to new endeavors. Of course, in the commercial TV realm, developing shows can differ as dramatically from the CTW Model as doing a pilot for *Prison Break* versus one for *Nova*. Shortcuts are taken, or layers of the process are removed, in part for budgetary reasons but in part to yield something with a different DNA. When it comes to baby and preschool content, the word *research* usually implies formative research, meaning feedback used to form new shows, as opposed to summative research, which sums up the effects of shows over a longer span and in retrospect. An academic in the field of evaluation named Michael Scriven is credited with coining the terms "formative evaluation" and "summative evaluation" in 1966. Only a few shows, notably *Sesame Street* and *Blue's Clues,* have undertaken summative research, and usually it is done in the pursuit of findings that will enhance promotional prospects. "I'm not sure what they got out of those tests," says a person who worked on *Blue's Clues*. "It always seemed like they would discover stuff that we did wrong. But it would be incredibly costly to actually go back and reanimate and rerecord those shows, so they would air anyway even after some small negatives surfaced in the tests." *Blue's* was the only show aside from *Sesame* to have each episode tested at least three times. Alice Wilder preferred to focus on formative research. "Why have to waste all that effort and money if you could anticipate, from interactions with kids in other focus groups?" she said. She recalled a *Sesame Street* episode that dealt with two kids squabbling and then starting to punch each other—a common problem among preschoolers. While the message of the show was about the need to avoid hitting, when it was tested after full production, kids started hitting each other, imitating the behavior they saw on the screen. As with the divorce episode, it never aired.

In some respects, although the CTW Model remains intact and upheld rigorously by plenty of people (especially at *Sesame Street* as it nears forty years on the air), it has been superseded by the pragmatic function of individual research consultants. These consultants—several of whom are former students of Dan Anderson—are generally given one-year freelance contracts. And once a consultant helps "make" a hit show, his or her services tend to remain very much in demand.

Consultant Laura G. Brown is a former middle school psychologist and private therapist who has helped shape preschool shows such as *Blue's Clues* and *Wonder Pets!* Given her track record, especially at Nickelodeon, she naturally was commissioned to help design the curriculum for *Downward Doghouse,* and was told the series could be a fit for the larger goals of Nick Jr., one of which has been to teach preschoolers how to cope with emotions. A small, warm woman who speaks with quiet intensity about her mission but also displays a generous sense of humor, Brown described Kai-lan as "that kid who knows how to help everybody else get along, or knows how everybody is feeling. In that sense, she is emotionally gifted." When *Downward Doghouse* went from being a diverting Web short being kicked around in development meetings to a full-blown, twenty-episode series, Nickelodeon brought in an unusually high number of consultants—six by last count. "Even our consultants have hired consultants," one executive joked. There were educational consultants (mainly Brown and Christine Ricci), cultural consultants (Jan Leu from the University of Washington), and language consultants (from the University of San Francisco). Getting all of them on the same page was as much of a challenge as getting ideas illustrated in Los Angeles, vetted by New York, animated in Taiwan, and then processed in Hong Kong.

If anybody could keep everyone on the same page, it would be the unsinkable Laura Brown. She graduated from the University of Pennsylvania and cites one of that school's icons, Martin

Seligman, as an influence on her work on *Downward Doghouse*. Seligman popularized a movement called "positive psychology," including his concept of "authentic happiness." A school Web page says Seligman's research "has demonstrated that it is possible to be happier—to feel more satisfied, to be more engaged with life" and claims at least seven hundred thousand adherents around the world. When we met, Brown had come from a meeting at Discovery Kids, whose curriculum is based on the power of optimism for preschoolers.

"I always liked narratives," says Brown, a native of the New York City suburbs. "I was not a *Sesame Street* watcher or a *Mister Rogers* watcher. I just never liked things that were explicit in their message. I always liked stories or relationships or music. *Magic Garden*, that was my show." Brown's three kids are six, ten, and twelve. For a time, they functioned as a convenient in-home focus group. Now, however, there is a slight problem. "My youngest really doesn't like TV," she says. "She's a very coordinated girl. She's physical and likes art. Sometimes I'll have to say, 'Sit down, I need an opinion.' 'But Mommy, I want to read! I don't want to watch TV!'"

In the world of preschool TV production, research is an old-fashioned game of relationships. Writers and producers meet researchers. Writers then rise to the level of creating shows and hiring staffs and they then hire the researchers they like. Laura Brown met Josh Selig, creator of *Wonder Pets!*, when they were both working on the show *Little Bill* and he eventually appointed her head of research for Little Airplane, the company he later started. Ricci, who worked on *Dora* and *Diego*, was brought in to help launch *Little Einsteins*—and, for that matter, organize research at the Disney Channel, after *Dora* producer Eric Weiner was given the task of getting *Einsteins* on the air and extending the Baby

Einstein brand into preschool. On a commercial level the dynamics involving these curriculum-designers-for-hire can resemble a form of the clinical trials run by drug companies. Funded by the corporations that are intending to distribute the product, the tests aim to support the claims that marketing departments are eager to make. "A lot of times, it's 'Oops, we'd better get some research to back up those claims,'" says one former senior executive at Nickelodeon. "And what they don't like to acknowledge is that one of the hardest things to do in media, and maybe in life, is to prove a causal relationship."

Dorothy Singer might take issue with that last statement. Along with her husband, Jerome, the Yale psychology professor has spent the past forty years or so examining children in day-care centers and determining how television can be an agent of improvement. They were inspired to follow that path by a visit to a day-care center. Observing kids pretending to be Peter Pan, they asked one of the teachers if it was because they had just read the book. "Oh no," the teacher replied. "They saw it on TV." Along with authoring many journal articles and books such as *The House of Make-Believe* and *Handbook of Children and the Media,* the Singers served as consultants on a show created by a Dallas schoolteacher that started as a video and took to the air once a mom who worked at Connecticut Public Television saw the spell it cast. The show was *Barney & Friends.*

Singer is a kind, grandmotherly figure (and an actual grandmother), who wore gray corduroys, a purple sweater, and black Birkenstocks on a recent school day, with her gray hair in a bob. The Singers' compact corner office on the seventh floor of Yale University's Kirtland Hall looks out onto New Haven's historic Grove Street Cemetery burial site of Eli Whitney, Noah Webster, and others) and the dome of Woolsey Hall. Though she is as indebted as anyone studying preschool media is to *Sesame Street,* she long ago spotted its limitations. "We always thought that *Sesame Street* was too fast-paced," she said. "If you put a child on the floor for and gave them a toy, let them play with it for a couple minutes, then took it away and gave them a different toy, then took that away and gave them another one, and so on, imagine what would happen. The child would become completely disoriented and confused and mistrustful of the new toy, while at the same time being attracted to the idea that there was a toy being offered." She squeezed her hands together. "Children really need time to pause and reflect. When I saw that Dan Anderson finally came around to that point of view, I shouted out loud. We kept saying, 'Slow it down!' and they have gotten a lot better in recent years."

The point Singer kept returning to was that children process TV differently than adults do. "If you've been in a preschool classroom, the teacher will speak in short sentences because if they tell a long story on and on, the kids can't follow. They will also sometimes put their hands on a child's shoulders or touch them in some way to guide them through a certain activity." In that same way, she said, it is crucial to have a live person or a voiceover explain to kids exactly what's happening, what's real and what's imaginary—as with Barney, the oversize dinosaur that led kids in song and taught straightforward lessons about interacting with others. "With all this animation, no one is doing that," she said. "But Fred Rogers showed how important that is in a show. He would always help kids understand what happened in the Land of Make Believe and that what was happening in his house or in the neighborhood was reality."

Singer was not familiar with *Downward Doghouse,* but from her description and writings about her work on *Barney,* the two shows share a number of striking aspects of the social-emotional curriculum.

"People found the show saccharine, but a child needs to have one hundred percent trust," Singer said. "They'll learn about cruelty soon enough. And I know very well from my private practice that when children have a stable home, they deal with challenges much better than those who are from broken homes. You'll do much better learning and coping with things life throws your way if you trust the adults around you. That's absolutely essential.

"In preschool, the social-emotional material should be what they focus on. The cognitive stuff, they can learn later. When they get to kindergarten, they'll learn the alphabet in one day. You have to give children ways to process emotions.... We don't allow children a true range of emotions in this society. You can't say to a child, 'Don't be angry!' You have to try to understand, and help them try to understand, why they're angry." She pointed to an example of helping preschoolers cope with emotions, an episode of *Mister Rogers' Neighborhood* that began with Rogers discovering his goldfish had died. "He tried to explain it to children and asked them, 'Do you remember him swimming? I have this wonderful memory of him swimming in the water and it makes me happy remembering that time when he was there in his bowl.' And the bowl stayed on the set, but they never replaced the goldfish."

Infiltrating the research apparatus, a realm full of complexities, yielded a basic understanding of its objectives and how it has evolved into such an essential component of preschool TV. But there was more science to fill in, mainly the question that had haunted me since Margot's birth: What is the bottom-line consensus among researchers about how entertainment affects babies and toddlers?

For answers, I traveled to Boston to spend a couple of hours with Michael Rich, a garrulous Maryland native and father of four who once worked in the film industry (serving as Akira Kurosawa's assistant director, among other things) before deciding to switch to medicine. Now a pediatrician, he runs the Center on Media and Child Health, a joint venture of Children's Hospital Boston and Harvard Medical School.

One of the center's essential functions is to centralize and make publicly available the thousands of research studies across many disciplines, addressing links between media and obesity, violence, smoking, attention, and many other issues. A growing number of the studies concerns babies and preschoolers, but there is a problem in trying to reconcile all the studies of those age groups, Rich pointed out.

"The research that's been done is in at least thirteen different disciplines," he said, quickly rattling off psychology (developmental, cognitive, and several other branches), gender studies, criminal justice, communications, sociology, anthropology, neurobiology, pediatrics, economics, and business (including marketing and advertising). "The volume of knowledge in any one discipline is so great that anyone working in that discipline can't keep up with all the research, let alone take a step back. What that means is that the knowledge base is fragmented or incomplete. We haven't laid out all the mosaic tiles and looked at the big picture."

That fragmented state of affairs hasn't stopped commentators, parents, and activists from sounding the alarm and claiming more definitive research than actually exists, I pointed out. The sharpest arrow in their quiver is a recommendation that the American Academy of Pediatrics (AAP) first adopted in 1999, in response to the wave of baby videos and preschool programming that had started in the previous couple of years. The recommendation urged parents not to expose children under two to screen media. Rich helped write the recommendation, which has been refined but never rescinded over the intervening years. One thing I have personally observed, and which was borne out in a 2001 study published in the journal *Pediatrics,* is that a minority of pediatricians offer guidance about media consumption during office visits. The study found 58 of 204 doctors surveyed taught about media exposure. Parents, too, are part of the disconnect. Only 6 percent of them are even aware of the AAP recommendation.

Rich agreed that there is "an education issue," but he offered a passionate defense of the recommendation's existence.

"Kids are learning all the time, from everyone they interact with," he explained. "In the first two years of life, the human brain triples in volume. It adds millions of neurons and prunes away millions of neurons. . . . One of the interesting things about the human being is that in order to end up with the most sophisticated brain in the animal kingdom, we trade off the fact that at birth we are the most helpless of all infants. Even higher primates are able to cling to mommy's fur and find the nipple. A human baby can't find food, can't get warm. It's completely dependent on other human beings. But our brains get to develop in the environment in which we must function, which is great. In those first two years, the basic architecture of our brain is being built."

He went on: "The studies to date are incomplete and imperfect. A good portion of why the AAP and others who have looked at this recommend against TV under two is not that we have a wealth of data showing it's bad for you, but because the data we have on early brain development indicates that three things are necessary to optimize brain development. The three that we know are good are face-to-face interaction with other human beings, manipulating your physical environment, and open-ended creative problem solving, like drawing on a blank sheet of paper, working with clay, or hitting a xylophone with a stick. Based on the fact that screen media cannot give you one of those three let alone all three, the biggest concern is about displacement, being in a suboptimal brain development space and losing the opportunity to develop a good, healthy brain. They'll be great at watching TV. If one is to be cynical or strategic, virtually every business tries to drive their brand loyalty and lifestyles younger. There is a huge advantage to teaching kids to be TV watchers earlier and earlier. As a business decision, it's a good strategy."

He had a point. Sometimes, I had already discovered, the line between what is advanced as research and what is marketing is difficult to discern, as a lucrative niche has been created by people hired to demonstrate the value of preschool enterprise. Spanning many different academic backgrounds, as Rich pointed out, they marshal evidence for a wide range of claims. Consultants for Cartoon Network prepared a compelling, densely footnoted forty-five-page brief demonstrating the importance of cultivating a toddler's sense of humor, and that appealing to it may unlock latent learning potential. A group of "experts," all from the West Coast, was rounded up (and paid) to endorse BabyFirstTV.

When I asked Alice Wilder, one of the architects of *Blue's Clues*, about the diluting of research by the propagating of "experts," she shrugged, "People need jobs. If you do this for a living and suddenly someone's coming to you and saying, 'We've read your work and think you're great and would like to include your name and picture in all of our materials,' it plays to the ego a little bit."

Given these discrepancies in claims, an obvious question is why there is no government initiative to study preschool media use, when the government does have initiatives in other arenas of education. A three-year-old bipartisan bill called the Children and Media Research Advancement Act, or CAMRA, would allocate $90 million over five years. Senator Joseph Lieberman of Connecticut reintroduced it in March 2007, but at last report it was still wending its way through Congress. Most people I interviewed knew it had been rattling around for several years and couldn't understand why it wasn't more of a priority.

"We'd be idiots not to welcome research," said Alice Cahn, head of Cartoon Network's preschool programming. "It'll be interesting to see what happens if CAMRA gets passed. If the American Psychology Association and American Academy of Pediatrics are as concerned as they are, why don't they put money up for research? Where are the academics getting funded to do this? Where's the National Academy of Science on this? Where's the Department of Education on this? . . . I do think that it's helpful to let parents know that there are issues, but to make blanket recommendations based on no research seems to be not as responsible a course of action as should be expected."

Speaking of blanket recommendations and responsibility, a widely publicized 2004 study linking TV viewing between the ages of one and three with significantly increased risk of developing attention-deficit/hyperactivity disorder, or ADHD, by age seven still rankles many preschool researchers. Lead author Dimitri A. Christakis, a pediatrician and professor at the University of Washington, has written widely about what he considers the insidiousness of TV viewing by children. That 2004 study, published in the journal *Pediatrics,* got an incredible amount of attention, landing on the front page of the *New York Times* and sparking a national conversation that continues to this day. The main flaw, many crit-ics point out, is that the study never screened for what kind of TV the child was watching. It could have been *Cops* or *Fear Factor* or *Sesame Street*. The appropriateness of the program was not taken into account. Additionally, the sample of roughly 1,300 kids aver-aged around three hours of TV a day. That is a lot of TV, but the only thing many parents heard was "TV linked to ADHD," and their anxiety intensified.

As parents are wont to do as conversations progress, Michael Rich and I got to comparing notes on the home front. I asked him about his practices at home, which were not a given in light of the ambiguities inherent in his profession. "I have a ten-foot screen in my screening room at home. I have a twenty-year-old and an eigh-teen-year-old and a two-year-old and a toddler. I've got my own little experiment going on. I got my oldest ones language tapes and they watched *Sesame Street* and a little *Mister Rogers*. My youngest son watches no screen media at all. I decided I was going to parent him with the latest information I have, whereas before I had less to go on. I noticed a phenomenal difference in his lan-guage acquisition. He loved books from early on. He could keep himself busy with books from the moment he could sit up. So we never faced that thing of 'I've got to put him in front of the TV in order to get a meal on the table or take a shower,' the need to use it as an electronic babysitter. My wife sits on an ethics research panel, the IRB [institutional review board], and she was looking at a study on language acquisition when our son was about eigh-teen months old. It said that the average child at eighteen months has twenty-six or so words. We said, 'Hmm, I wonder how many words Jason has?' We stopped counting at two hundred. How do you estimate someone's vocabulary? We never really thought about it. Although this is far from a scientific study, I am really glad I didn't sit him in front of a screen because it made him work harder to absorb the universe and figure out how to synthesize it and make it his own. It wasn't predigested for them."

I asked about his older kids.

"With one of them, it made him lazier as a student. He very much loves his media. He went off to college with a stack of DVDs a mile high. He has a passive attitude toward information and learning. But it's hard to tell if that's media or the way he was raised. The thing about media is that it's part of a whole complex life experience and you can't really point to it and say, 'This caused this.' That's the other place where this whole conversation gets derailed is that people want one-to-one causality."

That, to me, is an obvious flaw in many studies as well as in the unplug-all-TV proponents. "More work needs to be done on context," said Rosemarie Truglio, the head of research at Sesame Workshop. "We need to do more of those ethnographic studies that balance content with context to ask the question, 'What is the environment like when the child is exposed to television?'"

The environment of the Hayes household is something I had been obsessed with for some time when the flu bug hit like an atomic charge in April 2007. Coupled with unseasonably cold spring weather and record rainfall, it meant the four of us were cooped up for several straight days, passing around the virus and gradually driving ourselves insane. When we moved into our rental apartment at the Ansonia, a former hotel built in 1904 and where Babe Ruth, Enrico Caruso, and Theodore Dreiser were among the many famous long-term tenants, Stella and I told each other that the location and legend of the building would more than make up for a small space for a family (three rooms, about six hundred square feet). But the shadows overtook our world after Margot had a temperature that stayed at 104 degrees for several days, along with every other symptom in the book, and had been out of school for a two-week spring break (a biblical test of parental wherewithal).

I take particular note of this stretch of time because it reintroduced a character Margot called Stevie—a shortened form of a command she issued regularly when she was younger, "I want this TV!" Sick and unable to play or interact with other kids during the hours when she managed to stay awake, Margot watched far more TV than in her normal routine. It felt like a flashback to the good/bad old Toshiba days. We indulged her, in part because we felt bad about her suffering during the worst illness of her young life, letting her watch without restriction because I remembered the times over the years when I had been quarantined, growing restless with books, taking solace in the game shows and blessedly diverting daytime TV pabulum. Each answer to Final Jeopardy meant fewer thoughts about the bleakness of my phlegmy circumstance.

So Margot watched TV for unusually long stretches. A couple of the most intense sick days involved about three hours in the morning, then a short break, followed by a couple of hours in the afternoon with the DVD player and her favorites—*Dora, Diego, Wonder Pets!, Backyardigans, Max & Ruby.* When a promo would come on, promising a new program, she would perk up, reacting as if it were visiting hours in the sick bay. "*Wonder Pets!* is coming!" she would say, sounding lively despite the circumstances. Along with our feeling that it would comfort her to watch, we had our hands full with our son Finley, who was showing signs of catching the flu—a potential disaster for a one-month-old. Stella was breastfeeding, which was good for Finley's immune system but problematic for Stella, who was in pain and battling the flu herself.

One Sunday, it rained nearly eight inches in New York, the most in a single day since 1882, and Margot and I spent some quality time together. Finally back to her old self, she was teasing and joking and roughhousing. That was a huge relief. But as the old personality returned, so did her attachment to Stevie. In the afternoon, as rain lashed the windows, we resolved to play in her room. I had successfully turned off the TV after a "mere" two hours, and she then watched *Blue's Clues* on her little portable DVD player. The disc was called *Blue's Jobs* and one of the episodes that particularly interested her was about Blue going to the doctor. Another hour went by as I fed her lunch and read the paper. I told her the DVD had to go off and she didn't protest. Without the outdoors or a playmate or a babysitter to intervene, it was now just her and me (Stella was feeding Finley and catching up on sleep after a wakeful night). Margot negotiated a spin of her *Wonder Pets!* CD, sort of the methadone stage of the detox process. We colored for a little while and read her copy of *Highlights High Five,* a new preschool magazine. When the CD ended, I proposed playing with her blocks—traditional wooden alphabet blocks decorated with drawings of things that started with a particular letter. It was pure, creative playtime. First, Margot said she wanted to make a train out of blocks, then a plane, then line up all the animal blocks (alligator, bird, camel, etc.) outside her dollhouse, where she decided there was going to be a "big party." She was free-associating, looking at shapes, letting her imagination go. Many parents, if they are being utterly honest, will admit that it isn't always easy to get into this mind-set, attentional inertia without a screen. I have struggled at it, too, though on this occasion I was having a lot of fun, in no small measure because of how glad I felt that Margot was back to being Margot, soon to return to school with her friends. The rain clouds would part and the sun would reemerge.

After about a half hour with the blocks, something shifted in her. The ideas seemed to stop flowing. She dawdled over the blocks, hesitating for a long time when I would ask where she was going to put them next. Finally, with the abruptness characteristic of a three-and-a-half-year-old, she said, "I want to watch my DVD." I felt disappointed, annoyed, anxious. What did this mean? How could I let her return to her virtual world? Had her quota been reached? We were on a higher plane of learning through play. Why did she want to come back down?

I asked her, "Haven't you had fun playing with blocks?" Her response caught me short: "Uh-huh . . . but the DVD is better."

There it was. Try as I might, I wouldn't be able to compete with the layers of R&D that went into the winning formula of *Blue's Clues*. Blocks are pretty good, but you don't know the script. Maybe you'll lose your way and the train you're building won't have enough track or the party you're planning won't have the coolest animal guest list. Real life is unpredictable. Real life brings bouts of flu and sheets of rain. I had interviewed a dozen people connected to *Blue's Clues,* all of them likable and smart and articulate. I had studied Dan Anderson's persuasive case for why the show makes kids smarter. Since Margot first discovered the show almost three years ago, I have considered it a safe, enriching environment. Stella and I always wished there were more shows like *Blue's Clues.* Yet it was a little chilling to realize how the balance can get tipped between the real and the fantastical, how readily kids want to board that trolley to the Land of Make Believe. When researchers examined the effect of *Sesame Street* on kids' academic performance, they found that some of them complained that their teachers were not as entertaining as *Sesame Street*. And how could they be? Teachers are not edited, set to music, scripted, and acting. They are human beings and they do their best.

I tried to prolong the inevitable, prodding Margot to keep playing in her room rather than plugging back in. But eventually, I caved. She went back to the DVD. I told myself it was because she was still a little bit sick, that this was an exception, that it was just a security blanket that would be phased out again once she was completely well. I decided to watch with her, thinking that might allay some of the downside. I could ask her questions. We could share the experience, "co-view" a little. The first episode rolled. Steve was posing as a news reporter, delivering his usual patter in a CNN manner. "Why did you come over today?" he asked the viewer leaning in and looking straight at the camera. "To find clues!" a voice said. I asked Margot, "Why did you want to come over?" Her eyes never left the screen. "Don't talk," she said.

4

NO SWIPING

The Molding of *Dora the Explorer*

nother dawn with Margot arrived no more rosy-fingered than when the TV-watching era began. She was now almost two and the time was almost seven. The Toshiba was on as usual, but we had taken a break to kick a soccer ball. When Margot gave the ball a particularly deft boot, she raised her arms like Pelé and cried, "We did it!" I smiled at her display of pride. Without getting too after-school-special about it, her shout struck me as the essence of what I want her to do in life: celebrate her achievements and cultivate self-confidence. Looking at the show that had come on the Toshiba, however, I had the disconcerting realization that Margot had not come up with the phrase on her own. She knew when to use it and how to deliver it, but her uttering that sequence of words was about as organic and original as her saying "I'm lovin' it!" as we passed by McDonald's. She was merely mouthing one of the mantras of *Dora the Explorer,* the juggernaut Nickelodeon show that serves as a model for *Ni Hao, Kai-lan* and just about any show aiming to become a preschool hit.

When Sigmund Freud wanted to publish an article explaining his theories of psychoanalysis, he presented the case study of an eighteen-year-old woman whom he gave the pseudonym Dora. This is but one of the many ironic footnotes to the evolution of the perpetually seven-year-old animated explorer, who generates more than $1 billion in annual revenue from DVDs, CDs, toys, live stage shows, and a universe of more than two hundred branded products. Freud understood before almost anyone how crucial the toddler years are to the developing mind. In that spirit, understanding the preschool entertainment boom requires putting the animated Dora on the couch.

She began life, appropriately enough, in a theme park. And like any great American success story, she testifies to the power of the melting pot. In the early 1990s, Peter Schreck, a computer-savvy Canadian with a background in educational software, got a deal from Nickelodeon to develop interactive TV concepts. Geraldine Laybourne, who was running Nickelodeon during *Dora*'s initial development stages, had met Schreck in the early 1980s, when one of his inventions caught her attention—a banana-shaped wand that kids could use to interact with the TV when a situation arose that required audience input. When they got the right answer, it would beep. Even without the beeping and the hardware, the simple notion of appealing to kids for input was groundbreaking. Fred Rogers had been a neighbor and guide to kids, but Schreck saw a way to ask kids for help, which would draw a more intense response. "He was convinced he could teach kids how to read by replicating interactivity," Laybourne said. "He was a mad inventor. He was so exciting, this guy." She brought Schreck in to see her boss, Cy Schneider, an old-school adman who was intent on turning Nick into a little Tiffany channel. "He set it all up and then it didn't work and Cy threw him out of his office," Laybourne said. "About five years later, he came back, and he had figured out that if he studied enough kids, he could predict how they would respond and he could make fake interactive TV. I said OK, we'll give you access to four-year-olds." The move would have a profound impact on the next generation of preschool TV.

Schreck was assigned a trailer at Universal Studios Florida, where Nickelodeon then had production facilities, and proceeded to work on preschool shows for the nascent Nick Jr. label. The shows were called *Play With Me* and *Peter Penguin*. He animated the shows using computers—a novelty in the days before *Toy Story*.

He also established a regimen of testing that would provide him with constant feedback from kids—a "steady stream of four-year-olds," as Laybourne put it. That methodology was in sync with Nickelodeon's heavy testing culture and a twist on the CTW Model, and the network's new media department was eagerly anticipating the potential uses. This was the age of CD-ROM computer games, just before the Internet took hold as a permanent fixture of society. Angela Santomero, the young research coordinator who would go on to create *Blue's Clues,* was among those struck by Schreck's work. "They weren't shows that would necessarily merit being on TV," Santomero said. "There weren't characters or stories that were really developed. But still, there were educational concepts that were really salient." Plus, like Santomero's childhood hero, Fred Rogers, he was heightening the implicit suggestion of interactivity in television, the physiological reason why American viewers called Walter Cronkite "Uncle Walter" and welcomed Johnny Carson into their bedrooms. The notion of someone looking into the camera and speaking directly to the viewer has always proved to be magnetic, and all the more so in the realm of preschool. It explained the impact of *Mister Rogers' Neighborhood* or *Captain Kangaroo* or *Howdy Doody*. George Burns and Jack Benny also pioneered the notion of breaking the fourth wall to speak to the audience. But it had never been adopted as a regular format in animation.

Schreck's interest in interactivity came from his experience developing software-based learning systems for a division of Borg-Warner (the learning company that is now owned by Jostens). Aside from the company's official focus groups, Schreck would summon kids, with adult supervision, to his trailer. He would have one-on-one research sessions, showing them sequences of animal characters breaking the fourth wall to say words and sentences, separated by pauses and appeals to the camera. The pause in particular was a dramatic innovation, allowing children time to process information and develop responses on their own. It would become a formal feature of *Blue's Clues* and *Dora,* and can now be observed in at least a dozen preschool shows on the air.

Play With Me and *Peter Penguin* functioned as a modern update of the puppet shows and marionette plays that had been a children's entertainment staple for centuries. But given how readily computer animation could be manipulated by both creator and user, a door had suddenly opened to a puppet show on which the curtain would never have to fall. In a sense, Peter Schreck had developed the first anytime playdate.

"He was like a genius scientist in his lab, working on preschool," recalled Chris Gifford, one of the creators of *Dora.* "I used to love coming to see him work because he was so good at tweaking his work based on what he would hear from kids. I did worry initially about the potential for kids to feel tricked by the interactivity, by the fact that the characters aren't actually hearing what they're saying. But I spoke with [veteran kids TV researcher] Dan Anderson about it and he said kids love to pretend that the characters can hear them."

Neither *Play With Me* nor *Peter Penguin* became a series, but Schreck's work had far-reaching consequences. By 1999 and 2000, Gifford and the team developing *Dora* knew there was something powerful to build on. "Chris played the tape of the *Play With Me* pilot for me the first time we had a meeting and I felt like I had Tourette's syndrome," said Eric Weiner, one of the creators of *Dora* and now an executive producer of Disney's *Little Einsteins*. "It was done so powerfully that when Chris stopped talking, I wanted to yell out, 'Behind you!!' Some of it was the timing. It was so artfully done." Gifford said sound was one direct influence of Schreck on *Dora*. "I spent a lot of time with sound, figuring out when to drop out the music," he said. "'Bam-bum, bam-bum, bam-bum'—nothing. And then as a viewer you *want* to fill that space."

While his influence is evident in most of the successful preschool shows of the past decade, Schreck has faded from the preschool landscape, assuming the stature of a Philo T. Farnsworth, the man who invented television but never gained Edisonesque levels of fame. Many people who have spent years working in preschool entertainment don't even know Schreck's name. And that pilot tape that Weiner found so compelling is apparently gathering dust somewhere within Nickelodeon headquarters, for no one was able to find it after numerous requests. "He created the idea of interactivity, which became so ubiquitous. Everyone is doing it now," Gifford said. "He was gracious about it at the time. I wonder what he thinks, though, when he sees *Dora* everywhere. When you Google him, what do you find?" Barely a trace, I discovered.

Aside from Schreck, Gifford drew inspiration from a show he produced for Nickelodeon in the early 1990s called *Clarissa Explains It All*. The quirky sitcom aimed at school-age kids was noteworthy for centering on a young girl (played by Melissa Joan Hart, who moved on to *Sabrina, the Teenage Witch*) and for her disarming direct address to the camera and the viewer. "I always felt her interactions with the viewer really meant something," Gifford said. "Whenever she turned to the audience, she would bring something cool, some fantasy. That's something that has carried over to *Dora*."

When *Clarissa* ended in 1995, Gifford moved to New York, where he, Valerie Walsh, and Weiner began collaborating on a show known as *The Knockarounds,* centering on a band of problem-solving forest animals. The lead character, who would eventually become Dora, was then a raccoon. "Val had an idea for a treasure hunt show and I wanted to do an adventure show, so eventually we settled on a problem-solving show that would give kids tools to help them sort through all the things that come at them," Gifford said.

He then met with Albie Hecht, then Nickelodeon's president of film and TV entertainment, to pitch him on the idea. A colleague, Janice Burgess, came in with him to pitch a different show. Her idea became *The Backyardigans,* now a major preschool hit for the network. "I think it was the worst meeting of my life," Gifford said. "I was so down, my assistant brought me flowers." *Dora* remained in development hell.

Meeting with Gifford, it is difficult to imagine the down days. He is gregarious, laughs easily, and makes a lot of eye contact, despite being every bit the preoccupied producer. At a nondescript Midtown diner next to Studio 54 and the Ed Sullivan Theater, home to *Late Night with David Letterman,* he ordered fresh fruit, a bran muffin, and herbal tea, but barely touched any of it as he retraced the winding path both he and Dora had traveled. "I never do this, but I'm recovering from all the eating I just did in New Orleans," he said. He and his family have been making an annual trip to Jazz Fest, where "eating is a competitive activity," Gifford joked. "You're not only eating all this great food but you're looking around at what everyone else is eating and strategizing about how to get it." His lined, moon-shaped face, fair features, and light orange hair make him resemble a cross between Conan O'Brien and Harvey Keitel.

Gifford is known to kids-TV aficionados for playing the role of Danny on *The Great Space Coaster*, a half-hour series that now enjoys cult status for its irreverent blend of live-action slapstick, music, animation, and puppetry. He describes winning the role as a fluke. "They wanted professional musicians and dancers and I went down and auditioned with this broken-down bass and I somehow got my part. It was a dream job and I felt that it was the direction I was supposed to go." He got the audition as he was finishing a theater degree at Connecticut College. During college, he performed in a traveling children's theater group, "improv-ing a lot of bits and performing Shel Silverstein poetry, that kind of thing." Kevin Clash, a puppeteer who would go on to create Elmo on *Sesame Street*, also performed on the *Coaster*. He lent Gifford a little red-haired puppet for his one-man show called *Traveling Tales,* which allowed him to further hone his sensibility. "I'm not a professional puppeteer and I'm not funny, but I was funny with that puppet. I knew what to say to make kids laugh." The one-man show, plus his stint on the *Coaster,* led to a job at Children's Television Workshop and its science show *3-2-1 Contact*. A couple of years later, he made the jump to Nickelodeon. "I felt like I knew preschoolers and what was entertaining to them," Gifford said. "I loved the idea of trying to infuse preschool-appropriate things with getting the kids up and making it an active learning experience for them."

As a child, Gifford watched a lot of *Captain Kangaroo*, the CBS staple created by and starring Bob Keeshan, who had played Clarabell, the clown on *The Howdy Doody Show*. As I can attest from my own childhood viewing, *Kangaroo* was a pure rush. It emphasized entertainment more than education, which made it a refreshing counterpoint to the alphabet-and-morals fare on PBS. "Every kid loved when the Ping-Pong balls would fall" en masse onto Keeshan, Gifford said. "There was something naughty and rebellious about that but also something safe. Nobody was feeling bad about it."

Gifford knew his show needed to evolve further if the network brass was going to take a chance on it. Somehow, he had to raise the stakes.

"We debated a lot about making the raccoon human because we were worried about the ramifications," Weiner said. "We wanted her to be a brave explorer and somehow we felt that we had more license with an animal. We debated that endlessly and then decided to make her human. That seems fresher and bolder. So we crossed that bridge."

Gifford sculpted the lead character in the *Knockarounds* after his own daughter. She became an Irish redhead named Nina, whom Weiner described as "an ordinary girl who could solve any problem she encountered. She was a superhero by her persistence." Still in development, the show was soon retitled *Nina's Popup Puzzles*.

At this point, the creators were handed a radical new directive from Nickelodeon, one that would alter the fortunes of the show along with the landscape of preschool entertainment. The main character, they were told, needed to become Latina.

Brown Johnson, the veteran Nickelodeon executive who is overseeing *Ni Hao, Kai-Lan* as head of Nickelodeon Preschool, got the idea to change Dora's ethnicity after attending a trade conference called Children Now in Los Angeles. During the show, the lack of Latino role models on TV was repeatedly raised as a complaint.

"It's not just the skin color, it's the accent, the voice quality, the music, what the homes look like," Johnson said. "When I go to international conferences, all American TV just looks so American. All the homes are beautiful and tricked-out and the kitchens are all nice and the kids are all squeaky and shiny-looking and for a lot of people, life just doesn't look like that." Along with the environment, language would be an important component to the show. Bilingual preschool shows had existed before (among the first was *Teletubbies* creator Anne Wood's *Tots TV* on PBS). But *Dora* would increase the focus on language itself. "I wanted to make the ability to speak another language like a magical power and something to be really proud of," Johnson said. "So by making Dora a Latina girl, it gave us such a rich field to play in. We could explore technology, we could explore language, food, backgrounds, and animals and stuff that's culturally rich and authentic and it made it twice as interesting."

The one small catch: none of the creators knew more than a few words of Spanish.

"When we first started doing it, we translated every single word into English, and then we sort of slid into Spanglish, which some of our consultants, of which there are many, thought was a bad idea and some thought was a good idea," Johnson recalled.

"There was a big discussion about how integrated Spanish and English should be on the show. The truth is that is how a lot of Latin Americans speak Spanish and English. They intertwine the two."

Everyone at the network braced for some sort of fallout, given the wager on a Spanish-speaking heroine, but the feedback was largely positive from the moment Dora went on the air eight years ago. She is now generating $1.5 billion a year in revenue from hundreds of sources, including videogames, books, live shows, CDs, ring tones, and, of course, toys. Dora is a balloon in the Macy's Thanksgiving Day Parade and one of the characters that will entice families to stay in a planned Nickelodeon-branded hotel chain or travel to the Middle Eastern city of Dubai to play at a Nickelodeon theme park. In Manhattan, an entire floor of the Children's Museum is an interactive Dora exhibit thanks to a donation from Viacom, Nickelodeon's parent company.

The show itself has evolved slightly over the years, but its consistency is what has made it a commercial powerhouse. Ever-resilient and resourceful in her Mary Tyler Moore haircut, in each episode Dora is confronted by a series of tasks that she must complete—with the audience's help—in order to accomplish a larger, empowering goal established at the outset, such as freeing a princess or finding a missing toy truck. She and her sidekick Boots the Monkey consult their trusty map, which reinforces its role with an ultraredundant ditty (sample lyric: "I'm the map, I'm the map, I'm the map, I'm the map—*I'm the map*!!") and Dora's talking backpack, which magically contains provisions tailored to each journey.

The problem-solving story arcs and odd cast of characters are brought to life within a rigid storytelling structure that suggests a defanged, anti-Grimm fairy tale. In her essay "Narrative Theory and Television," Vassar film professor Sarah Kozloff points out that certain cartoons exhibit "blatant parallels" to the theories of Russian formalist theorist Vladimir Propp. Writing before *Dora,* she cites the 1980s series *She-Ra: Princess of Power.* In Propp's landmark 1928 book *Morphology of the Folktale,* he analyzed Russian stories and found seven character types common to all of them: hero, villain, donor, dispatcher, false hero, helper, and princess and her father. He also identified thirty-one distinct functions that recur in all stories (number 11: "Hero leaves home"; number 12: "Hero is tested, interrogated, attacked, preparing the way for his/her receiving a magical agent or helper [donor])."

In a typical *Dora* episode, the heroine's quest is always scrupulously outlined, the challenges made clear ("To get Baby Duck back home to his mother, we have to go through Purple Tunnel, across Crocodile Lake, and over Rainbow Bridge!"), and always the same handful of character-establishing theme songs. The animation style is no-frills 2-D, with motifs such as a floating blue cursor, picture-in-picture windows, and mouse-click sounds that underscore the Nickelodeon Web site's description of the show as a "computer-style adventure." As the introductory theme plays, the first image on-screen is a live-action shot of a child's bedroom, with the camera quickly zooming in on a computer monitor on a desk. The monitor screen fills with herky-jerky animations of Dora, Boots, Swiper, and the show's generic jungle background. It closely approximates a videogame, and that's exactly the point. The late-'90s zeitgeist of CD-ROMs, the emergence of the Internet, and the transformative power of technology are embedded in Dora's DNA.

Dora's quests are complicated by the mischief of Dora's nemesis, Swiper the Fox, whose adenoidal, Jerry Lewis–manqué voice undermines his cat-burglar getup of mask and gloves. "Swiper, no swiping!" Dora and Boots caution him in each episode. "Awww, man!" comes his reply as he snaps his fingers dejectedly. Swiper, to the adult viewer, falls well short of being the pure villain a child would encounter in traditional fairy tales or some of the early Disney animated features. He gets in the way of Dora and Boots and steals their stuff, but he doesn't exactly tie them to the railroad tracks. In several episodes, he comes around and works in collaboration with Dora and her friends, realizing the error of his ways. Even so, it is safe to say that the preschool world has never had a consistent foil as deliberately drawn as Swiper.

"That was a Chris Gifford idea," Weiner said. "One animal remained from the original group of animals in *The Knock-arounds* and it was Swiper. There's a power, going back to Big Bird, of the name being the word of what they're learning. So he's The Swiper. Another thing he did is that he came in and said his son thought he should say, 'Aw, man!'"

When I asked Weiner if kids ever reacted negatively to Swiper, he shared a remarkable story. "The very first time we took him out in still pictures, when kids were first exposed to him, they were wiggling in their seats, going, 'Ohhh,'" he said. "They clearly felt that he was going to eat them. They were filling in the blanks on what a fox does. We had to be a little bit careful about his teeth. But there was a watershed moment with the pigs when the three little pigs got loose because Boots forgot to lock the gate and we tested it in a preschool in Harlem and the kids were screaming out the responses and seemed to really be into it. It was like a rock concert. But then afterward, when they asked kids how it made them feel, close to one hundred percent said 'angry.' Not only that, but they started telling researchers things like 'I locked the door at home.' Scary things were coming up with them. And the researchers told us that we crossed a line. Preschoolers fill in that the bad guy is primal bad but you have to give them a fig leaf to hold on to that they can tell themselves that it's exciting but he just wants to take that one thing. So we added blue ribbons that the piggies got for being such good piggies. And then when Swiper was chasing them, we said, 'Oh no, he's going to take their ribbons!' So he stuck to his rules and then kids were back on the other side of the line of excited but not upset. Chris Gifford used to laugh about it all the time and talk about *The Jerk* and how Steve Martin says how much he hates those cans." He was referring to a scene in which Martin's character, while he is being shot at by a deranged sniper at a gas station, keeps insisting that the bullets are intended for a stack of oil cans.

One consultant on the show, Mary Grace Walker, said *Dora* was raising the stakes a little too high. But it was difficult for the creative team to throttle back, aside from making Swiper's teeth a little less sharp and his facial features a little kinder.

"I used to not care if kids were unhappy after an episode because how could we really know?" Gifford said, recounting a typical focus-group exchange. "'How does this story make you feel?' 'Sad . . . because my mom was mean to me today.' What do you do with that? But now I recognize that it's important that the takeaway not be unhappiness."

As I told Gifford, *Dora* has been a screen idol for my daughter. To me, though, the show remains as baffling as a foreign language slapstick comedy with no subtitles. One major reason is the start-and-stop sonic rhythms: the *Perils of Pauline* melodrama in much of the dialogue, the meandering, Casio-synthesizer incidental music, all of it then packaged with interactive moments of direct address to the living room. In one episode, Dora exhorts the viewer to help her make a car go faster, yelling, *"Vamos!"* After staring into the camera and blinking for a moment, she shrieks,

"Louder!!" Dialogue tends to be shouted rather than spoken. "I don't love it that they use their outside voices," Gifford concedes. "I don't want it to seem like they're yelling at the kids at home. It's not a gentle show in that way."

This emphatic quality perhaps explains why phrases from the show have crept into Margot's daily vocabulary—and not the kinds of catchphrases you might expect. As with the soccer moment, Margot often repeats simple things—"There it is!" or "What's that sound?"—that turn out to be derived verbatim from the show. A lot of parents have an automatically negative reaction to that mimicry, which I can understand completely. A friend of a friend, a magazine editor, told me recently about a trip to upstate New York with her four-year-old daughter. As they tromped around the farmland, the girl's voice dispelled the quiet. "Where do you look when you don't know where to go?" she asked. "The map!" Then came the familiar song, "I'm the map, I'm the map, I'm the map, I'm the map . . . I'm the *map*!" The mother endured it but thought later, "It gives her obvious pleasure, but I can't help but feel like something is taking up space. They've colonized her imagination."

That's how I felt initially, though after two years of investigation, I have also come to see some positive things about Margot's *Dora* fixation: She reacts energetically and verbally to the show, responding with answers when prompted and articulating choices she's making. She is also watching the world-conquering exploits of a seven-year-old girl who's a far better role model than Barbie or Cinderella. And whenever anyone starts to walk away with one of Margot's toys on the playground, she pulls out her trump card—"No swiping!" she'll say, holding up a hand like a superhero turning back a lightning bolt. Sometimes, when I'm feeling especially wary of the preschool machine, I fear that Margot repeating that signature line is inculcating adult concepts—paranoia, victimhood—too prematurely. But mostly I feel glad that Margot is sticking up for herself. The revolutionary flag motto "Don't tread on me" has morphed into "No swiping."

And there is a lot of scientific research that suggests that mimicry, known to be a fundamental development tool throughout the animal kingdom, plays an important part in unlocking toddlers' imaginative powers. Paul L. Harris, who was a leading developmental psychologist at Oxford and who is now at Harvard, has drawn on decades of experiments to conclude that "children are not bound by the physical world. They deem one thing to be another and readily imagine various make-believe transformations." By observing the world around them, Harris shows, they will adopt a "mommy" tone and tell their dolls to go to sleep, or even when playing with another small child, they adopt a "baby" voice and ask their friend if they can go to the bathroom. In other words, mimicry simply allows a child to manipulate the world during exploration, and the inherent egocentrism of the child will always allow them to shed a role easily. "The child talks while acting in a role, occasionally mimicking the intonation or accent of the chosen character," Harris wrote in *The Work of the Imagination*. "Role play depends on an active process of simulation in which the role player projects him- or herself into the make-believe situation faced by a given protagonist. Having fed that make-believe situation into their knowledge base, the role player can arrive at judgments, plans and utterances that are appropriate for the adopted role."

In order to sweeten the pot and clarify what exactly the high-pitched Dora was trying to teach, the creators of *Dora* decided (at the suggestion of consultant Valeria Lovelace, a former longtime CTW researcher and now a freelance consultant) to shape each episode to facilitate psychologist Howard Gardner's theory of "multiple intelligences." This overlay came fairly late in the process. Gardner, an eminent Harvard professor and author, believes that children learn best if educational materials incorporate eight distinct kinds of intelligence: linguistic, logical-mathematical, spatial, "bodily-kinesthetic," musical, interpersonal, intrapersonal, and naturalist. He believes existential intelligence, or the ability to contemplate one's own place in the universe, may be a ninth one.

Johnson and Weiner both recalled that when Weiner was the head writer, they developed what Johnson called a "matrix that had to be fulfilled. We had to have the Spanish, eight intelligences, she has to go on an adventure and have three choices. He said, 'I'm going to kill myself!' But his first script was about a big red chicken and it was hilarious. He had taken this little box filled with all these requirements and made something wonderful out of it."

The connection to Gardner was promoted by the show's producers and on the Nickelodeon Web site. Some people inside the network, especially those involved with *Blue's Clues*, seized on it as dismaying evidence of a network and a group of show creators who seemed so desperate for a hit that they would grab any current theory as an educational fig leaf. Unlike *Blue's*, a pedigreed show that had quickly established its place in the preschool canon, *Dora* played a little faster and looser, evolving in chameleon-like fashion from its animal roots to the loud and proud bilingual smash. The two shows, for several years beginning in 2002, were the twin engines of Nickelodeon, each piling up $1 billion in assorted revenues and giving the network the kind of brand identity its rivals can still only dream of. But internally, the emergence of *Dora* was something of a monkey wrench. With education and entertainment believed to be at opposite ends of the preschool spectrum, the perception was that *Dora* tilted pretty heavily toward the entertainment end. That's not a hanging crime, but in a sense the fulfillment of Geraldine Laybourne's original goal of cutting the green vegetables of early '80s Nick with a few tasty French fries. Like many sibling rivalries, it also centers on the charge that *Dora* was a mere copycat.

"They did a pretty good job copying us," said Alice Wilder, chief researcher for *Blue's Clues,* who said she was asked to consult on *Dora* but declined. "The Howard Gardner material was just trying to plug something in. In the classroom, his theory makes a lot of sense. But it doesn't make sense on TV." Gardner, in fact, never formally endorsed the show. He told me that no producer or consultant ever approached him and that to this day he has not seen a single episode.

Several *Blue's Clues* staffers said that while Gifford is well liked at Nickelodeon, where he has worked almost twenty years, at the point he was developing *Dora* he was, in one staffer's words, "really eager to just get his show on the air, no matter what it took." They blanched at what they saw as a disregard for basic child development precepts, as in the deployment of a character (Swiper) who, they said, modeled bad behavior for kids too young to understand it. Angela Santomero said she never let her daughters watch *Dora* because it is, among other things, "just too loud," a refrain I have heard dozens of times from people both inside and outside the preschool business. Arguably the only connection between *Blue's* and *Dora,* aside from the network that carries them, is Dan Anderson, whose consulting work on *Dora* extended his interactive-TV research that was the foundation of *Blue's.*

In the past few years, the balance of power that existed for so long between *Blue's* and *Dora* tilted heavily toward the latter. Production ended on original *Blue's Clues* episodes in 2005 and a spin-off called *Blue's Room* was launched featuring live-action puppets. It fared decently but seemed a muted presence on the network. Santomero and Alice Wilder left to go work on their new PBS series, *Super Why!* The plan as of 2007 was for them to work on occasional special movie-length *Blue's* episodes but not to have a day-to-day relationship at Nickelodeon. Meanwhile, *Dora*'s empire continued to expand.

Not surprisingly, the *Blue's* camp got a hearty laugh from a sharp-elbowed satire of *Dora* that aired on *Saturday Night Live* in March 2007. Flattered, so did Gifford. Under the banner *TV Funhouse*, the creation of comedy writer and Triumph the Insult Comic Dog alter ego Robert Smigel, the five-minute cartoon called *Maraka* follows a girl and her sidekick, Mittens. It brilliantly mimics the rhythms, bilingual bent, and shouted dialogue of *Dora*. When an eagle flies off with a penguin's egg, Maraka yells, "We've got to get the bird to put the egg down! Say 'put it down!' Again! Now flap your wings while you do it!!" She and Mittens put their hands on the back of their waists and flap their arms. "Flap your wings and yell. Don't question it. Just do it!! Louder!!"

The cartoon is punctuated by *Dora*'s braying imperatives and long, exaggerated pauses during which she and Mittens stand blinking at the camera. To anyone familiar with *Dora*, Maraka's dialogue is explosively funny, with lines such as "Get on your tummy! On your *tummy!* Do it, asshole!"; "Do you know why my daddy left me?"; and, imploring the camera, "Can you break a fifty?" After a flurry of action, Maraka booms, "Mittens saved Baby Penguin!" At the same high-pitched vocal register, she adds, "If Mittens chose to save Baby Penguin based on his beliefs and those beliefs were not in his direct control, does Mittens really have free will?"

Whatever her legacy in the broader culture, Dora continues to play a central role in our house. Margot lately has been pretending a Dora action figure lives in the small dollhouse in her room, along with two Little People figures (a knight and a fisherwoman) and the tutu-clad Zoe from *Sesame Street*. The little Dora is an exaggerated caricature whose head is the same size as the rest of her combined. Small, compact, and made from molded plastic, it fits very easily into her hand, but only fits through the dollhouse door if she turns and goes through sideways.

Late on a cold Thursday evening, Margot was preparing for bed. For a few minutes, she had been bringing the dollhouse to life, imagining that the fisherwoman was "the mommy" and Dora was "the baby." She was saying things such as. "Oh, baby, we have to take you to the doctor! We don't want you to get sick." Her murmurings were constant, repetitive, pleasing to my ear. Over a few months, as her vocabulary grew more complex and her grasp of language increased, Margot was able to create more complex scenarios. Often, as with a lot of kids, they were strikingly realistic. Stuffed animals going to school. Dolls having play-dates. Moms taking their kids to the doctor.

My usual tendency, as Margot's imaginative flights begin, is to refrain from actively playing with her, choosing instead to let her create situations and dialogue and sustain the whole scene herself. That's what I did on this occasion, though it got harder and harder not to intervene. Margot, lying on her stomach, knees bent, feet tracing figure eights in the air, used her hand to walk Dora around the rug, with the fisherwoman in the other hand. "Mommy, Boots has a hole in his shoe. We have to fix it. Can you fix it?" She mimed a sewing action. "Oh, great! Let's go! Wait a minute. How will we know where we're going? Dora, open your backpack. We need the map to tell us where to go. Say map. Say map!" The rhythms of her speech were now starting to approximate those of *Dora the Explorer,* just as with the soccer ball when she said, "We did it!"

Once the map had been consulted, an old familiar threat revealed itself. "Uh-oh, Swiper's coming," Margot said. "We have to stop him. Swiper, no swiping. Swiper, no swiping."

German child psychologist Bruno Bettelheim, in *The Uses of Enchantment*, argued that a child's fantasy life, as enabled by folktales and fairy tales, is crucial to his or her development. Though he was writing with school-age children in mind, his view has some applicability to preschoolers. Paul Harris has argued that a young child's imaginative play (contrary to the theories of Freud and Piaget) is not a phase to be viewed warily as a threat to overtake a developing young mind, but a conduit for continuous cognitive and emotional growth. In 1991, Harris and his colleagues published an influential study that examined the ability of preschoolers to distinguish fantasy from reality. They asked children ranging from three years six months to five years old to make judgments about three types of items: real (e.g., a cup), ordinary imagined items with real counterparts (e.g., a mental image of a cup), and supernatural imagined items with no real-life counterparts (e.g., a mental image of a witch flying through the sky). The results were overwhelming: 98.8 percent of kids understood that they could not actually see the imaginary items; 91.3 percent understood they were not, in fact, real. Preschoolers "appreciate some of the special qualities of mental entities, for example that they may be non-existent, impossible entities (e.g., pigs that fly)," the authors wrote. Stanford Professor Albert Bandura's theory of social learning also shows that being in a group helps an individual child discern real from imaginary.

Not everyone in the field agrees on how applicable Bettelheim is to preschoolers. But his conviction that fairy tales are not only valid but necessary was something I found appropriate to factor into my thinking about Margot and *Dora*. "Just because this life is often bewildering to him, the child needs even more to be given the chance to understand himself in this complex world with which he must learn to cope," Bettelheim wrote. "To be able to do so, the child must be helped to make some coherent sense out of the turmoil of his feelings. He needs ideas on how to bring his inner house into order, and on that basis be able to create order in his life. He needs—and this hardly requires emphasis at this moment in our history—a moral education." He added, "The delight we experience when we allow ourselves to respond to a fairy tale, the enchantment we feel, comes not from the psychological meaning of the tale (although this contributes to it) but from its literary qualities—the tale itself as a work of art. The fairy tale could not have its psychological impact on the child were it not first and foremost a work of art."

Can *Dora* be considered a work of art? I suppose that's where her whole existence has presented a challenge to me and a lot of other parents. There is a long history of popular entertainment engineered for kids grating on parents, almost by design, and *Dora* seems to fit right into that. But while the show has objectionable aspects to it for me and other parents, I have had to balance my adult misgivings hinging largely on aesthetics with my capacity to allow Margot to connect with it on her own. A study published in 2005 by Deborah Linebarger of the University of Pennsylvania tracked fifty-one children who were regular viewers of various preschool shows between the ages of six months to thirty months by giving them tests and interviews every three months. Among eight shows sampled, including *Sesame Street, Dora* was among the top ranked and was "positively related to both vocabulary size and expressive language use," in the words of the study. "Children will learn whatever they are allowed to view," Linebarger wrote. "It is up to us as parents, educators and producers to provide them with the best and most appropriate content possible."

Forget about the curriculum for preschoolers; there was a lesson for me as a parent in there. In the 21st century, whose "kidult" blurring of the lines sees grown-ups listening to "kindie rock," feeding their kids gourmet gelato instead of Good Humor, and dissecting the latest Pixar film, the notion of a tree house in our collective backyard with a misspelled sign saying "Kidz only" is a healthy thing

As Margot slowly tired and moved her playtime under the covers, she suddenly looked around. One of the little action figures from the house had gone momentarily missing. "Where'd she go?" Margot said, and I didn't even need to ask who. I retrieved the Dora figure from across the room and placed her onto the bed. Margot drew a breath in sharply, in a Christmas-morning expression of delight. "My Dora!" she cried.

Her Dora, I thought to myself. Exactly.

5

HOWDY DUTY

The Long Shadow of Early Kids TV

L ong before Dora came on the scene, there was another children's TV icon. He was, in fact, the very first to engage preschoolers on a mass scale, though it was with corny jokes and songs, not Spanish and multiple intelligences. His name was Howdy Doody, and his rise to dominance in postwar America defined the preschool landscape for the next twenty years. *The Howdy Doody Show*'s structure and mission, especially its puppet sequences and jokey songs, continue to echo to this day.

Along with Milton Berle, Howdy was the main reason there were 17 million TV sets in America by 1951, up from just 5,000 at the end of World War II. *The Howdy Doody Show* was not technically the first program aimed at kids, but it was the first widely successful, long-lasting network show to demonstrate that the kids business could be lucrative. And while it had no explicit educational or developmental aims, its run laid down a certain template for how to keep kids entertained.

Howdy Doody stemmed from a ranch-hand character that Bob Smith had invented for his morning radio show on New York's WEAF. Adopting a country bumpkin voice, he used the trademark phrase "Oh, ho, ho, howdy," and the name stuck. Soon after the character took off on the radio, NBC launched *Puppet Playhouse,* featuring Howdy, in 1947. When the character took off, the show was renamed *The Howdy Doody Show.* Early episodes featured a segment in which host Buffalo Bob would show the young children in the audience a cartoon, which became a show within the show. It was a money-saving way for the show to fill an hour of airtime. The cartoons were raucous, violent adventures replete with hammers to the head and other mayhem, a lot for the audience to synthesize given that some of its members—later dubbed the Peanut Gallery—were as young as two or three years old. Stephen Davis, a writer best known for his ribald, unauthorized Led Zeppelin book *Hammer of the Gods,* wrote a wryly engaging book about *Howdy Doody* called *Say Kids! What Time Is It? Notes from the Peanut Gallery.* It is in part a valentine to his father, who worked as a director on the show, as well as a memoir of growing up inside the Howdy experience. Davis recalls that, in the show's early days, Buffalo Bob would deliver a brief intro, then the lights would dim and the cartoon would light up the screen. In a sense, Bob was modeling behavior for the Peanut Gallery in years to come. He was training them to watch the screen, just as millions of kids at home were learning to watch the screen. His authority was absolute. When kids started to wave to the camera, Bob wheeled around and, without dropping his genial smile, said pointedly, "The next one who waves has to jump in the Doodyville pool." No more waves. Sometimes, Davis noted, the excitement would be too much, and the gallery would leave behind a few telltale puddles.

Aside from the cartoons, episodes were a loosely connected string of sketches all taking place in the fictional town of Doodyville, which was populated by characters such as Clarabell the Clown, Phineas T. Bluster, Dilly Dally, Flub-a-dub, Chief Thunderthud (with his retrospectively cringe-inducing "kawabonga!"), and Princess Summerfall Winterspring. The sensibility was pure Americana—Howdy's apple cheeks had forty-eight freckles, one for every state in the union. Buffalo Bob brought it off thanks to his years in broadcasting, musical aptitude, and ability to think on his feet.

Once *Howdy* revealed the robust potential of the kids-TV business—even in the days before DVDs, videogames, and theme parks—more innovations quickly followed. NBC's *Crusader Rabbit* in 1949 became the first popular, made-for-TV cartoon. In 1955, Bob Keeshan, who played Clarabell the Clown on *Howdy Doody* before leaving in a bitter contract dispute, started *Captain Kangaroo* on CBS, which ran until 1984 and then several more years on PBS. Soupy Sales, a popular kids' entertainer from Detroit, went national and inaugurated ABC's kids lineup in 1957. Disney's *Mickey Mouse Club* premiered in 1955.

An important societal shift was under way in the 1950s, of course, that helped radio and television cultivate such avid child and family audiences. Children were being developed as consumers. Even the very fields of child psychology and child development, which began to take shape in the early 20th century in the wake of Rousseau, Darwin, and Freud, grew at first not purely as academic disciplines but as adjuncts of the consumer marketplace. E. Evalyn Grumbine, one of the field's early pioneers, gravitated in this direction, attaining fame for her 1938 book *Reaching Juvenile Markets*, a primer aimed at advertisers and mechandisers. Many researchers and academics studying marketing and advertising tried to apply theories to consumer behavior, which continues to a significant extent today as academics are drafted to help develop television shows.

One of the many striking things about *Howdy Doody* episodes, viewed several decades after they first aired, is the amount of time dedicated to commercial promotion. A "Vote Howdy" campaign on the show in 1948 positioned the freckle-faced marionette as a presidential candidate, and only kids could cast ballots, which were found inside specially marked packages of Wonder Bread. Buffalo Bob would spend up to three minutes touting the "zip and zing" that a slice of Wonder imparted. He even plugged that organically nutritious food known as Hostess SnoBalls. Once the show itself proved a juggernaut, *Howdy* tie-ins multiplied—dolls, records, books, lariats, beanies, and the like.

As children's shows proliferated, their effect on viewers became the subject of dim conjecture. The magnetic pull of this early programming was unmistakable. The debut of *Puppet Playhouse*, the original showcase for Buffalo Bob and his marionette pal, had been the biggest magnet yet. "In the middle-class home," a reviewer in *Variety* wrote, "there is perhaps nothing as welcome to the mother as something that will keep the small fry intently absorbed and out of possible mischief. This program can almost be guaranteed to pin down the squirmiest of the brood." As Stephen Davis describes the reception of the earliest broadcasts, "The children of the affluent Northeast were catatonic. Thousands of mothers made dinner in tranquility. Thousands of postwar Baby Boom fathers put their feet up and read the paper."

Psychologists from Stanford University, gathering research in the 1950s for the watershed study published in 1961 as *Television in the Lives of Our Children*, assumed a stance that seems a little paranoid even by the standards of that unsettled decade, yet also oddly prescient. Preschool viewers watching television, as with bedtime stories, are "in bondage to broadcast schedules and parental availability and, of course, to someone else's sense of pace and emphasis," the authors wrote. "It is worth noting that the child is introduced to the mass media almost wholly as fantasy and as audiovisual experiences. These are, of course, the child's most pliable and impressionistic years. The way he begins to use television may well help to explain why the idea that television is for fantasy is so deeply ingrained by a child that he often has the greatest difficulty in thinking of educational television, let's say, as a proper use of the medium." The National Television Review Board, with the endorsement of *Reader's Digest* magazine and the national Parent Teachers Association, put *Howdy Doody* on its "objectionable list," deeming the show "loud, noisy and confused." Pediatricians started diagnosing a mix of indigestion and hyperactivity with the name "TV tummy."

Many early productions purveyed a strong sense of wonderment and even obsession with the new medium. A show called *Jim and Judy in Teleland,* produced in 1949 and 1950 and syndicated in 1953, attempted to fulfill the fantasies of the first "TV generation" by showing Jim and Judy gaining access to Teleland by climbing right into their television set. Similarly, *Winky Dink and You,* a crude stab at interactive television, combined cartoons and commercialism in a prescient way. Kids would buy a *Winky Dink* art kit, which included a piece of clear plastic vellum to be laid directly onto the TV screen. Crayons in the kit would then be used to color along with host Jack Barry, who narrated a simple story as the camera stayed on a static shot of a character. The show became somewhat notorious because so many kids would, at Barry's invitation, begin drawing on the TV screen. The problem: Many did not have their *Winky Dink* kits handy and quickly ruined the family TV set. Despite these logistical snafus, Barry was onto something with *Winky Dink*. In terms of interacting with the audience, *Winky Dink* could be thought of as an early ancestor of *Dora the Explorer.* In a similar way, *Winky* was in sync with the era's merchandising boom, which had started with Mickey Mouse watches in the 1930s and caught on in the late 1940s. By the end of the 1950s, it had become a $200 million market.

Much of the programming that aired in the 1950s and '60s was locally produced. The economic model of television was radically different from today's, with stations in individual markets producing shows to fill the schedule and making a profit from selling local ads. Today, with national advertising having long ago dwarfed local markets, the most efficient way for local stations to operate profitably is to serve as network affiliates. Stations produce perhaps a few hours of local news but little else in the way of original programming. In place of syndicated fare such as *Judge Judy* or *Wheel of Fortune,* decades ago shows such as *Romper Room* and *The Soupy Sales Show* found their audiences locally before (in many cases) getting a national pickup.

The blossoming of television as a medium is not just an academic story for me, but a rather personal one. My dad has worked for almost fifty years in broadcasting, more than half of that in television, so ours was in many respects a TV household.

Having been charmed along with the rest of their baby boom peers by the small window onto an electronic world, my parents embraced TV in the broadest sense, as a means of social connection, stimulation, and entertainment. Nonetheless, we weren't representative of the gloomy average American home, where the TV blared for seven hours a day; it typically was on far less, as I remember. But during the years my older sister and I were growing up, our family's reasons for entering that phase of attentional inertia became, at root, completely personal. Because my father's livelihood was television, we watched not just to be diverted or hipped to the latest trends. We watched as a military family would fly a flag on the front porch.

Starting in his teenage years, my dad read news and spun records on the radio. He always maintained the aura (and worked the long hours) of a dedicated newsman who could never pass a wailing fire engine without wondering where it was headed. His outgoing greeting on our answering machine had the urgent tempo and crisp diction of a dispatch from the field, something all my childhood friends noted with delight. When I was a toddler in Detroit, the slogan of WXYZ, as with many ABC affiliates then and now, was "Eyewitness News." It suggested that at any moment, day or night, someone somewhere could be seeing news happen and that news could end up on the air. A perfect mantra for Dad.

There were even times when Dad, although he mainly worked behind the scenes producing and directing, appeared on the air. One especially memorable time was when I was about five and we were living in San Francisco. Due to a strike by a couple of his station's main unions, employees classified as management were called upon to serve as replacement reporters and anchors. My dad very capably stepped into that role, even to the point of reporting from a helicopter. Another time, he was asked to anchor the six o'clock news and my older sister and Mom and I gathered around the TV. Suddenly, he appeared and we got a unique charge out of seeing him in our living room, a virtual presence where he was usually a physical one.

At one point, when we lived in Detroit, a camera crew from WXYZ had captured me on a day of heavy rain out in my backyard making mud pies, displaying the intense concentration of an Iron Chef contestant. The footage was used as a backdrop to the nightly weather report. I remember that I looked at TV a little differently after that. It is hard to say with certainty, but looking back the question of reality versus what appears on television was first introduced to me at that time. I still believed in Santa Claus but I somehow got the sense that TV was a construct.

Swiss child psychologist Jean Piaget explored the way babies and toddlers develop a sense of what is real in his book *The Construction of Reality in the Child*. While many of Piaget's tenets have been challenged, to me some of his findings in this area remain as valid now as they were when he was writing in 1954. "During the first months of life, the child does not dissociate the external world from his own activity," Piaget wrote. "Then gradually, as progress is made in the intelligence which elaborates objects and space by spinning a tight web of relations among these images, the child attributes an autonomous causality to things and persons and conceives of the existence of causal relations independent of himself."

I have wondered, as a consequence of investigating Margot's relationship to television and writing this book: Did I become an avid TV watcher as a child because I was somehow trying to get closer to my dad? It's kind of an armchair-psychology rationalization, but it also seems fairly legitimate as a theory. At the same time, seeing my dad on TV or myself on TV from an early age may also have wound up intensifying my anxiety and mistrust of TV as a parent because I am inclined to see the artifice and worry about Margot devoting so much time to something so artificial. I don't have the same faith that my parents have, faith that what Margot is watching is harmless at worst, edifying at best. My sister and I often laugh about the time when she got a rise out of my parents by insisting—as devoted conspiracy theorists have—that the 1969 lunar landing was a phony event shot on a soundstage, an elaborate cover-up of the truth that man has never walked on the moon. They both were furious at the notion, which underscored their rationality but also positioned them as true believers in television.

One theory that could explain my dad's TV faith is that his early years coincided with the origin of the medium in America. He was born in 1940 and witnessed its introduction in the late 1940s and early '50s. For kids growing up in southern Ohio, television was a glimpse into the future and the sophistication of New York City. Decades after pulling in those first TV signals, my dad wound up working at WNBC in Rockefeller Center, the very place where so much early television began, including *The Howdy Doody Show.*

As I began writing this book, I asked my dad to try to remember some of his first experiences watching TV. He was a little fuzzy on details, remembering mostly that his family was the first in the neighborhood to have a little black-and-white RCA set. Most screens at that time were only about five inches across. He remembered watching one show with his dad: *Kukla, Fran & Ollie.* Produced in Chicago, *Kukla,* which began as a segment on the NBC show *Junior Jamboree,* was not expressly for preschoolers, and in fact my Dad was about ten when he started watching it. Roughly analogous to contemporary animated shows such as *The Simpsons,* it could be enjoyed by young and old because of its sardonic wit and breezy sophistication. Watching episodes for the first time was an amazing experience on two levels, offering insights into the birth of the medium and my own father's formative TV experiences.

The rhythm of the show is relaxed, with the camera remaining steady, and long, semi-improvisational riffs unfolding at a leisurely but engrossing pace. In one scene, Kukla spoofs Dave Garroway, the first host of NBC's *Today* show, donning thick-rimmed glasses and explaining that the imitation is easy because "he just sort of stumbles around the set." Later, as he leafs through *Life* magazine, Fran, his human co-star, asks him what he's reading. He quips, "An article about the high-brow, the upper-middle-brow, the lower-middle-brow, and the low-brow." After one of the show's staple musical numbers, which showed off Fran's velvety voice, Kukla said, "I just defy Fred Waring [then a popular TV bandleader] to get something better!" Ollie then ate the sheet music, prompting Kukla to quip, "Now he'll know it by heart."

Even the commercial plug became very much a part of my dad. They devoted about four minutes to a game-show-style product showcase of sponsor RCA/Victor's console that had a five-inch TV screen and could also play a stack of ten 7-inch, 45 RPM records. When my dad went to work at 30 Rockefeller Center, NBC was owned by RCA and the building was the RCA Building. He often visited the company store, which offered discounts on RCA products. Our first VCR, our TV sets, and innumerable other household electronics bore the brand that my dad had in his house growing up and on his favorite TV show.

In examining the chronology of how children's TV evolved, I was intrigued to discover that at the very same time of all the activity in Doodyville and my father's hometown of Portsmouth, Ohio, another 1950s TV pioneer was emerging in Middle America: Fred Rogers. A native of Latrobe, Pennsylvania, Rogers returned home in 1951 after graduating from Florida's Rollins College with a degree in music composition. He got hired by NBC in New York as an assistant producer for *The Voice of Firestone*. With some experience under his belt, he returned home again and developed a show,

The Children's Corner, for WQED, a Pittsburgh TV station that went on the air in 1954. The show enjoyed a short run, including a Saturday morning spot on NBC. Galvanized by the experience and determined to carry forward some of the ideas into a more fully realized setting, Rogers spent several years developing what would become his lasting legacy: *Mister Rogers' Neighborhood.* It debuted on PBS in 1968, preceding *Sesame Street* by a year.

Mister Rogers always acknowledged a show from the early 1950s that influenced the *Neighborhood.* It was *Ding Dong School,* which originated in Chicago but eventually became a national NBC series. Its creator, producer, and host, Frances Horwich, was known on the air as Miss Frances. Dressed in the prim style befitting her background as a teacher, she sang the theme song in a sturdy, Kate Smith–like warble. As she sang, the screen showed a simple black-and-white image of a tolling bell. "I'm your school bell / Ding, dong, ding / Boys and girls can hear me ring / Every time you hear me ding, dong, ding / Come with me to play and sing."

The key innovation of *Ding Dong School,* taken further by the warm and more overtly loving Rogers, was Miss Frances directly addressing the young viewers of the show. Given the limitations of the medium, and the sense that it was live theater done in front of cameras, there were plenty of shows whose hosts looked straight at the camera. But Miss Frances spoke to the children in the audience as if they were sitting at her feet. In fact, she was alone on the set, which was a Spartan little space where Miss Frances would place a few objects—household items that could double as toys, musical instruments she could demonstrate. Her demeanor was steady and stolid. Seen from across the decades, the show's appeal is hard to grasp. To an adult viewer, Miss Frances seems less comforting than somewhat menacing with her pressed lips and tight bun hairdo giving her a controlled, almost Nurse Ratched–like intensity.

Signing off one program just before Labor Day weekend, she offered unadorned moral instruction. "Yes, have fun together," she intoned. "Have a good time. But when you have a good time together make sure that it's real, that it isn't just something that someone has cooked up as an idea and has kind of forced it on the other fella. Because when you cook up something, it doesn't work always. It takes everyone to plan together."

Operating in the full-color TV world of the late 1960s, Fred Rogers had infinitely more tools at his disposal. His show took place in a real-looking home, not a spare TV set. An ordained Presbyterian minister, Rogers behaved as a missionary of love and acceptance, though he managed the remarkable feat of never injecting his faith into the show in an overt way. In the context of early television, he was among the very first to understand that child viewers needed to be taken seriously as developing beings. He honored their every emotion, expressing through song, fantasy, and plain talk that it was OK to be experiencing whatever feeling they had. In thirty-three award-winning years on PBS, the show pretty much covered the whole emotional gamut. It was one of a small handful of great shows over the years, and Rogers made his audience feel completely safe with a soothing voice and measured tone that mesmerized many kids, including me.

In my travels working on this book, I asked everyone I could about Rogers—why he remains such a singular figure. "When I was raising my kids, my older son couldn't stand to watch *Sesame Street,* because it's too fast, but he loved Mister Rogers," said Marjorie Kaplan, head of Discovery Kids. "He's living a child's life. That world of make-believe is that kid world where you take a chewed-up sock puppet and a plastic dinosaur and a toy train and they all talk to each other. As an adult, you don't remember that until you see how your parents saw it."

Some people agreed with that dichotomy, saying that kids chose sides between the two PBS powerhouses. But I personally found them to be complementary, and both took early TV in a completely different direction from where it had started after World War II.

My prized possession from early childhood was an autographed photo of King Friday, ruler of Mister Rogers' Land of Make Believe. My father, perhaps unsurprisingly, was never fazed by how much TV I watched as a toddler. "I think you actually came out much smarter because of all the TV you watched," he said. "You're way ahead of where a lot of people in my generation are." I asked him why he believed that. "*Sesame Street* taught a lot. It's so brilliant and you learned from it, plus the other shows that were out there." I probed more, but he kept returning to the same assertion. Like everyone engaged in the effects-of-TV discussion, he was unable to point to definitive proof. It once again came down to faith; he believed that engagement with television could enhance my cognitive abilities.

Some research has backed him up on that point. A longitudinal study completed in 2005 by University of Chicago economists found that viewing of *Sesame Street* is "closely associated" with academic achievement. Kids who watched performed better in math and English compared with nonviewers. I wonder about my dad's conviction that I came out ahead when I hear him rail about how television, the medium that nurtured his dreams as a child and provided him with a rewarding life, has been disappointing him in recent years. The industry is riddled with reality-show obsession and managerial dysfunction, expressed by an abandonment of news. It's a completely reasonable critique, especially from someone who has poured so much of himself into it. But as I survey the generations—his, mine, and now my children's—I wonder what it will mean if he loses his faith.

Tom Junod memorably profiled Fred Rogers for *Esquire* in 1998, speaking for many of us facing the fact that the guiding presence of our childhood years was entering his twilight. (Rogers died in 2003.) The cover story, headlined "Can You Say 'Hero'?," saluted Rogers for continuing the fight against the medium's inevitable decline. "Mister Rogers is losing, as we all are losing," Junod wrote. "He is losing to *it*, to *our* 24-hour-a-day pie fight, to the dizzying cut and the disorienting edit, to the message of fragmentation, to the flicker and pulse and shudder and strobe, to the constant, hivey drone of the electroculture—and yet still he fights, deathly afraid that the medium he chose is consuming the very things he tried to protect: childhood and silence."

Junod relates the story of Rogers accepting a Lifetime Achievement Award at the Emmys. From the stage, he asked the crowd to take ten seconds to think of the people who had helped shape their lives. "And then he lifted his wrist, and looked at the audience, and looked at his watch, and said softly, 'I'll watch the time,' and there was, at first, a small whoop from the crowd, a giddy, strangled hiccup of laughter, as people realized that *he wasn't kidding,* that Mister Rogers was not some convenient eunuch but rather a *man,* an authority figure who actually expected them to do what he asked—and so they did."

Rogers and Buffalo Bob and Miss Frances were all vested with a kind of authority only the first audiences of TV could give them. In a TV appearance in the 1980s, kids TV host Soupy Sales—by then known to me and others of my generation as merely a game show regular—reflected on the sea change over the generation that had passed since his eponymous show was launched. "TV changed everybody's life," he said. "When I was growing up, you had to be home for dinner at five-thirty or six and you talked to your mother and father, brother and sister about what happened during the day. As soon as TV came along, people were having dinner in front of the TV. They weren't paying attention to what anyone said. It became an individual thing." In 1975, at the precise time when I was most in thrall to Captain Kangaroo, Keeshan observed, "TV is a convenient baby sitter and parents too often use it that way. By the time a child starts school, he has seen about 5,000 hours. That's time taken away from peers and parents at a crucial period of development. The effect has to be negative."

If one of the 1950s pioneers of kids TV could reach such a state of anxiety about how much TV kids are watching, just imagine the feelings of conflict and guilt in today's parents. In the absence of information and reasonable medical guidance for parents, the boom in preschool entertainment offerings has been accompanied by a national cri de coeur. Even advertisers are seizing on the sentiment. Panasonic has launched a Bring Back Family Time campaign—to plug high-definition TVs. As I talked to friends and parents of my daughter's friends during research for this book, I was struck by the intensity and prevalence of Keeshan's sentiment. *The effect has to be negative.* Many of these people had watched TV early on and remember their parents being dazzled by it in the medium's earliest days. But their discussion of it carried little nostalgic warmth; instead, it was anxiety-provoking and fraught with issues of parental responsibility, learning, work, and family.

In the baby group we belonged to during Margot's first two years of life, our friends had diverse philosophies. Our friend David, a writer, was weaned as I was on *Sesame Street* and *Mr. Rogers.* He found that his son, Sebastian, became transfixed by videos that were not even intended for him. During frequent night wakings, David started watching a top-selling video by Dr. Phil–like pediatrician Harvey Karp called *The Happiest Baby on the Block,* which depicts proper techniques for swaddling and soothing mewling infants. That was followed by a title called *Baby Signs,* whose popularity resulted in Sebastian learning sign language by the age of six months old. "Ruth feels like we're slipping when we let him watch TV, but I don't," David says. I agree—both parents are avid readers, engaged in the community, possessed of strong ties to family. Sebastian could do far worse, even with the TV on. In fact, Stella and I often felt a weirdly competitive twinge when Sebastian hit certain cognitive milestones—reading, recognizing letters—before Margot.

David takes pride in those accomplishments, but they don't minimize his anxiety over entertainment. "The funny thing," he said, "is that all parents have something where they draw the line, like 'We draw the line at *Barney*' or 'We draw the line at *Teletubbies.*' It's a way for them to feel like they have some control over the flood of stuff that's available. But it's harder and harder to. It is a little insidious when you see how widespread the imagery is. Elmo is on Sebastian's diaper, it's on the floor of the supermarket where you buy diapers. It's on every rattle." He can't shake the unsettling feeling of his son being somehow neutralized by TV. He mentioned psychological studies that have determined that adults prone to depression can "bottom out" while watching TV. "I see that a lot with Sebastian," he said. "He can't fully articulate it, but I really believe he feels worse."

Juliet, a professor of women's studies at the University of California at Los Angeles, believes moms and dads react differently to that guilt complex. "For me, it doesn't necessarily turn on the question of developmental consequences," she says. "It's more of a feeling that I'm being a bad mother, that I could be doing something else with my child."

Before getting pregnant, she shared a TV-free apartment with Ali, also a UCLA professor. "We felt really strongly that when we had a child we would not let them watch. We made lots of judgments about people watching TV and letting their kids watch TV, especially babies." After holding out for a year with son David, she started feeling pressure from other parents and relentless marketing campaigns. "So we started experimenting at night," she said, almost as an addict might confess to her first hit. "We were lucky that David wasn't waking up terribly early but he would stay up at night. Now, when guests are over or even on a lot of other nights, it's as much TV as they want. We have cable, TiVo. Roxy [David's little sister] has grown up with the TV on all the time, sometimes two hours at a time, though they're not always watching." Still, she defended her choice as something of an act of faith. "The way your kid looks while he's watching TV isn't necessarily comforting," Juliet said. "But the stimulation is being registered. I was worried about this when David was a baby and I looked at one study that found there was a strong correlation between watching TV and scoring better on tests. I think there's a way to become a very discerning viewer and get a lot of cognitive stimulation from TV."

In New York, we have become good friends with Victoria, a staunch opponent of a lot of mainstream media, especially for her three-year-old son, Nikolai, a playmate of Margot's. "It's brainwashing," Victoria said, with an exasperated look. "Everything on the screen is connected to something that you're expected to buy. This materialism is needless." Born and raised in the Black Sea city of Odessa, Vika emigrated to the United States in her late twenties and did not consume TV as my wife (like Vika, a Russian

Jew from what is now the Ukraine) and many other immigrants do, as a way of learning English and immersing themselves in American pop culture. She generally frowns when her husband, Michael, lets Nikolai watch DVDs, but she related an incident that, to her, demonstrated the spell cast by preschool entertainment. It was when her son watched *Here Come the ABCs,* a video based on an album of songs about the alphabet by quirk-pop band They Might Be Giants. (Sample track: "C is for Conifer.") "He ran around for days saying 'Giants! Giants!'" she said. "I couldn't believe he knew all the letters, and I think it may have been because of that video." She shook her head ruefully, her expression depicting the parent's dilemma of wanting to raise intelligent, curious children but also not wanting to plug them into an anytime playdate.

Her expression changed when I asked Vika whether she was watching anything at the same time American toddlers were being introduced to *Sesame Street.* Her gentle, moon-shaped face softened into a wistful look and she recalled Cheburashka, who was the Soviet Mickey Mouse rationed to viewers in fifteen-minute doses by the three state-run television networks, starting at the same time as *Howdy Doody,* after World War II. "I loved that there was something on that screen for me," she said, sounding for all the world like a charter member of the Peanut Gallery.

6

STORY TIME

Kai-lan Meets Her Audience

A handful of three-year-olds sat in a cross-legged semicircle in the middle-class Los Angeles suburb of Glendale, the setting for James M. Cain's 1941 noir novel *Mildred Pierce*. The Spartan preschool room had a stained blue rug, fluorescent overhead lights, and a few scattered stacks of wooden blocks. A frizzy-haired, petite woman named Cecily Miller greeted them, and got ready to tell them a story. "This is the kind of story," she tells the toddlers, widening her eyes for effect, "that you can talk during, or stand up or move around or dance or sing, whatever you feel like doing." An anticipatory hush fell over the room. It was story time.

Except Miller is not a teacher. She is the research manager of *Ni Hao, Kai-lan*, formerly *Downward Doghouse*. The storytelling session was, in fact, a focus group for the show, in which she read text and dialogue while displaying twenty-nine TV-screen-sized placards that depicted scenes distilled from an episode of the show. It was the fourth focus group so far for *Ni Hao, Kai-*

lan, which was expected to have fully produced episodes on the air in less than a year. Producer Mary Harrington, a tall, well-coiffed Bostonian and former vice president for animation at Nickelodeon, sat in the back of the room. From her years based at "Nick," as the most-watched U.S. cable network likes to call itself, she knew the research process intimately, though she had never worked on a preschool show. "I'm falling back on a lot of what we did with *Rugrats,* which was a huge hit with preschoolers. I really know character and comedy; that's what I'm bringing to this." She added, "We have consultants working with us to make sure it's appropriate for two-year-olds."

Harrington, creator Karen Chau, and head writer Sascha Paladino were in Glendale to find out what kind of show they had and in what direction they could move next. After winning a coveted series order, they were essentially building a show from the ground up, and doing it across languages and cultures to boot. On this April day, under a thick marine layer (a local euphemism for smog), they were trying to get a clear picture of what approach would connect with kids.

The trio observed the three-hour proceedings, which were broken into distinct tellings of the story for three-, four-, and five-year-olds. Some of the placards had Velcro-attached layers or moving parts that made them look like pages from a pop-up book, to approximate the feel of an animated episode. A video camera on a tripod in the corner ran continuously, its low whirring drowned out by the hum of traffic on the nearby Ventura Freeway. The episode introduced Kai-lan, a five-year-old Chinese girl; her grandfather YeYe; and a menagerie of animal characters, among them a frog called Mr. Hoppy, an albino lemur named HoHo, and a pink rhino, Roxie, who hovered in midair, suspended from a red balloon. Adults in the room outnumbered kids 6 to 5.

Nearly every episode starts with Kai-lan saluting the sun in a traditional yoga pose (hence the yoga reference in the show's original title, *Downward Doghouse*). The episode being tested on this particular day starts with Kai-lan finding Grampa working in the garden. She admires his hat and tries it on. When she discovers it's too big for her, she decides to make her own and to organize a Chinese tradition: a hat parade. All of Kai-lan's animal friends make hats for the parade, but some tension arises when HoHo is found to have copied the hat made by a panda named Rintoo. In the end, Rintoo learns the lesson that, as Grampa says, "When someone copies you, it can mean they liked what you did."

"OK, now we're going to talk about the story," Miller told the semicircle. "Before we all talk as a group, I'd like each of you, one at a time, to go answer a couple of questions with my friends Jasmine and Michelle" (she indicated two assistants with clipboards on either side of the room). The kids did as they were told. As two of them headed to the sides, Miller asked the remaining three a few innocuous, stalling questions about pets. ("Oh, you have a goldfish? What's its name?") On the sides, Jasmine and Michelle showed each child a narrow horizontal strip of cardboard depicting an emotional spectrum. "How did the story make you feel?" they asked each child. The strip had five slots, for "very happy," "happy," "OK," "sad" or "angry." Most of the fourteen children pointed at the "happy" end of the spectrum and no one reported being angry.

After the individual data were collected, Miller really started earning her pay. The final—and most crucial—phase of the session is usually a discussion about the nuts and bolts of the show that she moderates. The goal is to collect a comprehensive set of impressions, so Miller never corrected or interrupted; she only gently cajoled or led where appropriate. She was preternaturally patient, comfortably handling the antsy, wriggling, attention-hungry preschoolers while pleasantly eliciting their opinions. One five-year-old wandered around so much that she effortlessly—and with the soft but swift touch of someone very experienced with young kids—swept him into her lap. "You're going to be my special helper, OK?" she said. He was delighted not to budge the rest of the day.

The full three hours were videotaped and would be analyzed by researchers—facial expressions, response times, attitudes—and written up a week later in an official report. All Miller had to do was keep all the kids participating and motivated. It was working so far.

Her questions were meticulously scripted. Glancing smoothly down at a printout to remind herself of her lines, Miller ran through a standard series, occasionally holding up new placards that showed a close-up of a single character. Who did you see in the story? Who was the girl? Who's this? What did she do? Did you like him? What's a *mao-tze*? Then, the capper: What was your favorite part of the story?

Group dynamics were a factor in the room, but not nearly as much as in focus groups of tweens or teens, where the "queen bee" syndrome can sabotage the results. For young kids, this process is more manageable because each age group has just a handful of children, selected to span the sexes and races. Of course, one four-year-old (Audrey) shot a hand in the air every time a question was asked. And a three-year-old (Genevieve) was so quiet that Miller had to really work to draw her out.

Sometimes, the answers were surprising. "What did Rintoo do that you didn't like?" Miller asked, holding up the panda's picture. "The monkey knocked down his hat," said a girl named Lan-an, referring to a moment that never happened. In the back of the room, the team members exchanged looks with their eyebrows raised. Sometimes the folly of polling such a young group was unmistakable. "How do you say 'hat' in Chinese?" Miller asked. "Hat in Chinese," came a three-year-old's Abbott & Costello reply.

During breaks between age groups, the team members huddled briefly to review the results. "They really *got* the story," Paladino said. There was a murmur of agreement, but some issues were raised about elements that didn't go over so well, for instance, a music cue and the pacing in another section. The structure of *Ni Hao* resembles that of *Dora the Explorer,* with long pauses built into the script to allow for child participation, a technique first pioneered by Nickelodeon's *Blue's Clues,* where children guess the clues in part based on prompts by Joe, the host, which he gives by pausing for the answer and prompting viewers with an encouraging look. Unlike those other shows, however, *Ni Hao* has what the team describes as an "emotional curriculum." Kai-lan and her friends provide models for viewers about how to identify emotions and consider the others' feelings. It's a tall order for a small audience, and the creators craved a sense of whether the kids at these focus-group sessions were actually absorbing any of those lessons.

Toward the end of the last session, sensing that the kids' energy was flagging, Miller led them in a "cool-down" that lasted all of sixty seconds. "Rub your hands together! Put your hands on your head! Hit your head! Hit your head! Hit your shoulders! Shake out your face!" She got a lot of participation from the group. They just seemed happy to have the chance to move around.

After wrapping up at the school, the team piled into Harrington's black BMW for the drive to Nickelodeon's animation headquarters in nearby Burbank, where they would have a conference call with executives in New York to "debrief." Embedded in an industrial section of the San Fernando Valley, the ten-year-old building bursts with color and whimsical design. Clusters of cubicles for each show are decorated to suit the palette and style of that particular show. Animators and writers have lockers encased in dry-erase boards, the better to custom-decorate regularly. The *Ni Hao, Kai-lan* area is festooned with red and yellow Chinese lanterns hanging from the vaulted, loft-style ceiling. "They're grouped in threes and sixes," explained Chau. "According to [the Chinese spiritual principles of] feng shui, those are lucky numbers. Although eight is actually the luckiest number." Harrington affected a half-joking nervous expression. "So why can't we have rows of eight?" she asked. "We probably should," Chau shrugged, "because that's the absolute best luck you can have." Before the day was done, the lantern shuffling had already begun.

Over a lunch of takeout Thai food, the group digested what the target audience had revealed and responded to. They did this again later before the conference call with New York, at what the group called a "casual debrief" for the whole Burbank staff. "They like the physical stuff," noted Harrington, an expert in animated comedy. "We should do a lot more of that." For example, she added, a set of silent characters called the Peking Mice "are underutilized. I expected more of a reaction to them." Chau agreed. "They're definitely one of the quirks of the show and they're definitely very kid-relatable." "Are you making a pun with their name?" Harrington asked. "I've always thought they were 'peeking mice' and that we should see them peering around corners." Chau nodded, scribbling in her notebook. "The kids love that. That'll be something for the three-year-olds."

The mood was definitely upbeat as the group sensed progress, or even just a tangible reading of where they stand. Basically, they knew at that point they were at least in the arena. All of the work to follow would just be about getting closer to the target. Miller made special mention of the high comprehension scores for the core theme of the episode: that imitation is often a sincere form of flattery. They also appeared to have hit on a trait that must be part of any preschool TV show—one touchstone moment or "formal feature" that consistently occurs in a certain way and at a certain time in each episode. Dora, for example, consults her map. Joe sits in the Thinking Chair to solve *Blue's Clues*. In the hat parade episode of *Ni Hao, Kai-lan*, there is a passage where Kai-lan is shown in close-up. Rintoo has just complained about HoHo copying his hat design. Kai-lan sings a short ditty whose tune resembles "The Itsy Bitsy Spider": "There's always a reason why / we gotta, gotta try / to find the reason why / Rintoo stomped away!"

With the last line adaptable to each episode's plot, the team believed that moment could become one of the show's signatures. In order to drive home the emotional curriculum, there needs to be that extra point of emphasis. The challenge is to properly calibrate the moment so that it's paced and worded just right. At the debriefing, for example, Miller questioned, based on the initial feedback, whether preschoolers could distinguish "proud" from "special." A line of YeYe's dialogue, "You should feel very proud of what you made," did not resonate with the kids in Glendale, but when Miller keyed on the word "special," there was a spark. It would be almost two years before *Ni Hao, Kai-lan* reached the air, but there was already some clarity about its mission. As Paladino put it, "We kind of have a checklist of interactions and beats now that we want to hit in every episode. . . . One of the difficulties of preschool is that there's an A story only, not an A or a B story, so if the audience isn't connecting to the A story, you have nothing to fall back on."

There was only one problem with *Ni Hao, Kai-lan* in the spring of 2006; it hadn't truly become a full-fledged show. Most Nickelodeon series are green-lit based on a pilot of seven to eleven minutes in length. Usually that length allows the pilot to map out each character and suggest interactions and educational opportunities. The *Downward Doghouse* shorts jumped off the screen visually, and the character of Kai-lan was unquestionably viable. But what exactly would her adventures be? What would be the point? What would she teach, aside from cultural awareness? "The shorts were really charming, but they really only had glimmers of character in them," said head writer Sascha Paladino. "We needed time to develop the characters, to figure out who was who and how they were going to put across the educational content, the language, the culture," he said. "We started writing scripts way too quickly." In that respect, Paladino said that with more distance from that day in Glendale, the team decided that it was "an important day in the evolution of the show." As further evidence of how compressed the process was, a year later, in April 2007, the show's "bible" was still being finalized. A document typically about ten to fifteen pages that spells out the mission of the show, all the characters, the point of view, the visual style, and every other basic element, a bible is usually written and signed off on at the start of a show going into production, though it typically gets revised and updated on a continual basis. The accelerated pace of how *Ni Hao* was acquired and put in motion meant that the fine-tuning had stretched on for more than a year.

The team quickly began to see what they were up against: the complex challenge of threading Mandarin, Chinese culture content, and emotional lessons into twenty episodes without a cast of fully fleshed-out characters. Another curveball: Departing from the protocol on many other preschool shows, researcher Christine Ricci insisted on replicating the technique she used on *Dora* of having the writers come up with a storybook outline rather than a full script. That storybook would be the first thing tested, as in the "hat parade" episode in Glendale, and then that feedback would inform the first draft of the script.

Once the group realized that they were in danger of falling far behind schedule, they discussed moving the broadcast date back a few months. The network was reluctant; with a show that could become the next *Dora*, they didn't want to make any rash moves. But rather than risk a rush job that would be criticized for mishandling the unprecedented Chinese elements, Nick Jr. decided to postpone indefinitely. The show was removed from the official schedule.

Back in Burbank, while relieved to have a bit more breathing room, the team attacked the series, deconstructing it in order to put it back in a better order. One thing sorely lacking, Chau decided, was a male character. Paladino agreed. "We needed at least one more character, and we decided an alpha male would really help improve the energy of the show and open up story possibilities. So that's how Rintoo was born." Rintoo would be a tiger. Paladino suggested the name, which he borrowed from an old friend who is Bangladeshi. "*Rintoo* doesn't actually mean anything, but this guy was always kind of rambunctious and that's the quality we wanted the character to have." Chau thought a white tiger would be especially meaningful, given that the rare animals are revered in China. The network objected, pointing out that HoHo was white and that too many white animals would dull the palette. Brown Johnson, head of Nickelodeon Preschool, also ordered a change in a sequence in the hat parade episode. Instead of a bakery called Mr. Fluffy's Cakes being run by an octopus named Yan-

Yan, she preferred a polar bear in order to avoid any confusion with Oswald, a big blue octopus who is the star of his own Nick Jr. series.

Those were fairly superficial details, and the script seemed to be on target with its deeper content, especially the emotional material. The episode focused on jealousy, one of the "hard emotions" that individual episodes would try to hit, among them bragging, sadness, anger, pride, listening, sharing, teamwork, and disappointment. Some of the emotions would be covered twice during the course of the season.

In addition to the clutch of consultants that all had to communicate, there was another point person who had gotten involved. "Alex Chen, who is head of Nick China, was having a big problem with 'Chinglish,' as she calls it," Johnson said. "By having some characters only speak one language and others speaking another language, you sort of ghettoize them a little bit. Whereas if everyone speaks a little, it becomes more normalized and feels more comfortable." In this way, the show had been harder to calibrate from a pure language standpoint than *Dora,* which deployed "Spanglish" in a more natural way. "I'm friends with this couple, she's Turkish and he's from Senegal and so she speaks Turkish to their daughter, he speaks French and I come over and speak English and she follows," Johnson said. "They just code-switch, they know who to talk to in what language. It's amazing."

What had been starting to dawn on everyone even before the test in Glendale was just how disparate the Chinese and American cultures are. *Dora* was certainly not easy to get on the air, but it was beginning to look that way in comparison with producing *Ni Hao.*

"The way the generations treat each other is quite different. The Chinese-American experience is that Chinese immigrants might have come from a communal living situation, one big family, one patriarch, give up individuality for the greater good. When they come to America, the kids go to high school, it's all about self-expression and individuality. At school, they experience things one way and at home they're being told to live a completely different way. Certainly I think there's a big culture clash that happens there. This show, when we started, grandfather was the primary caretaker of Kai-lan, which is not unusual. But he's also her confidant. We had some consultants say, 'That would never happen. You should have a bluebird or something who's her confidant.' But Karen really liked the idea that he was there."

For Chau, the realizations about the cultural divide were both personal and professional. "The Chinese don't hug and say, 'I love you,'" she said. "And they aren't encouraged to speak out and be individuals." An earlier focus group in Chinatown in Los Angeles revealed what the show might be able to tap into—and what it would be up against. "One girl burst into tears and ran out," Chau said. Paladino added, "And no one answered any questions!" Chau continued, "It's true, they just moved their hands a little bit but then they looked around and felt self-conscious and stopped."

Johnson said she was amazed to learn how deep the differences ran. "Affection between parent and child can be expressed by telling them they're not good enough, they'll never amount to anything, they're so terrible," she said. "In a way, that might be their backwards-talking way of saying, 'We love you, we're really proud of you.' Karen says he knows her dad really loves her when he starts criticizing her."

Consultant Jan Leu, a professor at the University of Washington who consulted on the Chinese cultural aspects of *Ni Hao*, "kept making the point that the goal is neutrality in her culture," said Laura Brown, one of the show's educational consultants. "In America, happiness is the goal. It's in our Constitution. So we set out to create as many calm, happy moments as there are excited, happy moments."

The group shaping Kai-lan into a relatable heroine seemed to be in unanimous agreement about what qualities she needed to have in order to be true to Chinese culture, the curriculum, and Chau's initial vision. Still, a question loomed: Would American kids respond? As estimable as Nickelodeon's track record has been, it was far from certain that placing such a pricey risk on China would pay dividends. It was difficult for many adults to absorb Chinese culture with any sophistication, let alone children for whom *Ni Hao, Kai-lan* would be one of their first narrative experiences. And there was the deeper level of probing emotions. What if little kids could not be persuaded to learn to examine the feelings they were having? What if they preferred simple adventure yarns instead? "That's why this has been the hardest show I've ever produced," Mary Harrington said.

7

TOYETIC

How the Toy Aisle
Became a Preschool Battleground

I magine lying on the beach on a blazing hot summer day. When you close your eyes, you hear a swirl of sounds: children shouting, people chatting, waves crashing, seagulls crying, music pulsing, paddleballs making their muted *thwok* as they hit wooden racquets.

Now imagine that discordant mosaic of sound reverberating in a vast space, the volume dialed up substantially, and the aroma of hot dogs and nachos filling the stale air, and you have some idea of the experience at the American International Toy Fair. The 103-year-old trade show is held in New York's Jacob K. Javits Convention Center. Geographically, the aircraft-hangar-like halls of Javits are just a mile or so from the city's historic epicenter of toys, the International Toy Center, which long sat on 23rd Street and Fifth Avenue across from the landmark Flatiron Building at the southwest corner of Madison Square Park. Spiritually, however, it's a world away. A neoclassical building, the toy center is as old–New York as it gets. In the early years of the fair, yo-yos and red wagons were the draw, and it seemed more appropriate to invoke Baudelaire's famous observation that toys are "a child's first initiation to art."

At Javits, it ain't about art. Strobe-lit thirty-foot banners hang from the rafters, while electronic bleeps and bloops and floor-rumbling video clips on plasma screens trumpet the latest product launches and tie-ins with film and TV properties. These licensed products account for about 25 percent of the toy industry's $22 billion in annual sales. There are 100,000 toys at Toy Fair, of which 5,000 are brand-new. Retail buyers from thirty countries schmooze with everyone from mom-and-pops to multibillion-dollar conglomerates. As marketing expert Erik Clark puts it, Toy Fair is "a unique feature of the toy business—a group of grown men and women deciding ten to eighteen months in advance what a three-year-old will want to buy when he is five." No one under eighteen is admitted to Toy Fair. Perhaps because of the clarity that affords—no photo ops of babies playing with specially designed rattles or toddlers doing battle with the latest videogame—one can learn a great deal about modern baby and preschool enter-tainment here . . . if one can focus amid the din.

Ni Hao, Kai-lan was not one of the stars of the 2007 or 2008 Toy Fairs. New shows on Nickelodeon and many other channels are customarily on the air for eighteen to twenty-four months before toy lines get rolled out. The purpose of that lag time is to avoid incurring manufacturing costs for a show that doesn't con-nect with enough viewers to turn a profit.

Nevertheless, Toy Fair is crucial to those seeking an under-standing of the business and cultural realities of a preschool pro-gram. For most consumers in the United States and abroad, the toy aisle is where the Kai-lans of the world will live forever, or at least until next Christmas. If she succeeds, Kai-lan will be played with by many more people than will watch her. At the same time, Toy Fair is also known as a place of discovery. Here, in 1997, Julie Aigner-Clark walked from booth to booth with a copy of a video she had just shot in her basement outside Atlanta. It was called *Baby Einstein,* and its success began when Aigner-Clark button-holed a woman from The Right Start, a specialty retailer, read her name off her name tag, and gave her a personalized pitch to consider stocking the video, which she eventually did. Toy Fair is now an essential stop for anyone hoping to reach consumers from birth to five years old, for two main reasons: one is that the Census Bureau projects that this segment of the population will grow by 5.5 percent by 2010; the other is the acronym KGOY. Not a West Coast radio station playing only Pat Boone, KGOY is marketing shorthand for "kids getting older younger," a pronounced form of age compression that continues to unsettle everyone with a connection to toys. Essentially, it means kids who used to discover Barbie or G.I. Joe at seven but who are now doing so at three are done with them by kindergarten, at which point they start playing videogames and instant-messaging their friends. The shift is starting to show up in the sales figures. In 2006, action figures plummeted 9 percent, while youth electronics soared 22 percent.

Many in the preschool business fear the overall toy business, which has had static sales for the past several years, is suffering because of the same impulse that is compressing the age of television viewers. "Two to five is now the sweet spot for toys," says Sherice Torres, Nickelodeon's senior vice president of consumer products. "Kids need to have something aspirational. So while the kids watching a show might be a little older, preschoolers are going to start playing the videogames or watching the DVDs.

They're going to want something that's a little older than them." For that reason, older-skewing draws such as *The Simpsons* or *High School Musical* sell a lot of merchandise to preschoolers who don't watch the shows. One recent survey by the toy consultancy Funosophy found that the top show-related toys for boys ages two to five were from *SpongeBob SquarePants,* a show that none of them could likely fathom. Toy icons among older groups blatantly target preschoolers, as in the case of Hasbro's Super Pal Spider-Man, a plush doll that utters phrases far gentler than the dialogue spouted by Tobey Maguire's PG-13 crime-fighter. "Can a hero get a hug?" he asks. "What a great day we had!" Ads for the doll announce "two parent-friendly modes" and urge preschoolers to "cuddle up with your spider pal and rest for tomorrow's adventures."

Mindful of this new age imperative and how much the general toy business is struggling, Toy Fair itself has altered its course. To reflect a priority shift, the motto for the 2007 edition was "Inspiring Growth" and the posters and literature scattered around the Javits Center featured a multicolored pinwheel-like flower suited to a preschool classroom. Although major manufacturers from Hasbro and Mattel down to smaller mom-and-pops book display space and use the three-day show as a vast media opportunity, the focus has changed. In earlier years, Toy Fair was a venue for dealmaking involving toymakers, license holders, buyers, and retailers. Today it is largely a media platform. Widely covered by the mainstream press, it is especially appealing to TV networks looking to fill airtime with a segment about what kids will be asking Santa for that Christmas. Retail sensations from the Furby to Tickle Me Elmo, which created retail panic during past holidays, had their first exposure in February at Toy Fair. The 2008 edition also figured to be newsy, in the wake of major toymakers recalling batches of toys produced in China, many of them tied to preschool brands such as *Bob the Builder,* due to the discovery of lead in their paint or plastic. The scare dominated headlines in the late summer of 2007 and presented parents with a holiday season conundrum. The layers of that dilemma would increase manifold were little Kai-lan to take toy form.

Toys and children's entertainment have had a cozy relationship since at least 1932, when Kansas City adman Herman "Kay" Kamen started to roll out the first licensed merchandise for the Walt Disney Company. He struck deals with Lionel toy trains and Ingersoll-Waterbury clocks and watches. The appeal of Mickey Mouse, whose popularity had soared since his screen debut in 1928, spurred sales and helped the licensors avoid bankruptcy during the Great Depression. The licensing fees, in turn, helped Disney start making feature-length films. Anticipating the branded youth culture soon to come, the Cleveland *Plain Dealer* described a child's experience in 1935: "In his room, bordered with M.M. wallpaper and lighted with M.M. lamps, his M.M. alarm clock awakens him, providing his mother forgets! Jumping from his bed where his pajamas and the bedding are the M.M. brand, to a floor the rugs and linoleum upon which are M.M. sponsored, he puts on his M.M. moccasins and rushes to the bathroom to have the first chance at . . . no, you're wrong . . . at the soap made in the Disney manner, as are also his toothbrush, hair-brush and towels."

Given the intense competition today, the lure of discovering the next Mickey or Dora is too great to resist. Even Sesame Workshop, a nonprofit, has to deflect criticism about its mission now that Elmo and other characters are generating $46 million in licensing revenue, not just from toys but across categories from diaper packages to juice boxes. "That money helps us go into parts of the world where childhood literacy and poverty are terrible problems and really make a difference," said Sesame CEO Gary Knell. "Without the money from all the licensing, we wouldn't be able to keep those promises." When government funding was drastically reduced in the early 1990s, Sesame Workshop responded by expanding into theme parks, stage shows, and further into toy stores. In his book, *PBS: Behind the Screen,* Lawrence Jarvik accused *Sesame Street* of becoming "an infomercial for 5,000-plus licensed products."

The reality is that every producer of kids shows is feeling the presence of a new elephant in the room. "At meetings now, no matter what the show is, people are talking about making sure shows are 'toyetic,' and I never used to even hear that word," says a consultant who has worked on preschool shows for several networks. I heard that word myself at Toy Fair in 2007. Brian Goldner, chief operating officer at Hasbro and an executive producer of the movie *Transformers,* told me how delighted he was that director Michael Bay had made an "extremely toyetic picture" (not an entirely surprising outcome for a movie based on toys). The word itself is bizarre, a blunt perversion of *kinetic* or *synthetic* that allows people to comfortably express a corporate longing that a piece of popular art also opens onto a vast horizon of business opportunities. What would its antonym be? "Toyresistant"?

Bernard Loomis, perhaps the preeminent architect of the infrastructure connecting children's television and toys, coined the term in the 1970s. A veteran of Mattel, General Mills, and Kenner, he played a pivotal role in several initiatives that signaled a shift, as he put it, "from consumer-driven, where the customer decided what he wanted, to being a consumer-communication business." In the 1950s, that meant taking the embedded toy ads of *Howdy Doody* and *Winky Dink and You* a step further with specially produced spots that aired during kids' programs. (Loomis helped influence Mattel's decision in 1955 to devote its entire ad budget of $500,000 to producing spots to air during kids' shows.) In the 1960s, the next leap was producing a show for ABC called *Hot Wheels* that was quickly seen for what it was: a thirty-minute commercial for Mattel's toy cars. Then, at the dawn of the 1980s era of deregulation, he championed the syndicated show *Strawberry Shortcake,* which would join *Care Bears, He-Man,* and a raft of others as product-driven cartoons where the product explicitly came first. *Transformers,* for example, was fully owned by toymaker Hasbro, which licensed the toys to a Japanese animation company, which produced a TV series that aired in syndication and stimulated toy sales.

A lot of preschool veterans see a rosier picture than in the 1980s, though companies are marketing themselves to children who are savvier in the ways of technology and of marketing itself than any prior generation. "Kids are more powerful than ever before," said Leigh-Ann Brodsky, president of Nickelodeon & Viacom Consumer Products. "They are able to get content and make it their own. That's a scary thing for people who own properties, but it's also good for us because kids are more invested in the process and feel more connected to it. Now it's up to us to come up with strategies to take advantage of that." Jessi Dunne, executive vice president of global toys at Disney, added, "There used to be a formula, but not so much anymore. Now, it all comes down to play patterns"—which is trade jargon for what kids like to play with and how they play with it. "We are going through a sea change," says Al Kahn, CEO of 4Kids Entertainment, whose properties include the Cabbage Patch Kids and the Teenage Mutant Ninja Turtles, who were recently resurrected in a modestly successful computer-animated film. "It's age compression and also age distraction. If you could either control one action figure or control ten thousand figures on a screen, which one would you pick?"

Before her busy Toy Fair week began, Brodsky took a few minutes to meet with me in a conference room at Nickelodeon's Times Square headquarters. Toys and merchandise were laid out on several tables, where the future for *Ni Hao, Kai-lan* could arguably be glimpsed in the lines for *Dora* and *Go, Diego, Go!* Dora now has more than two hundred officially licensed products, from a Dora jeep to a Dora castle to Dora cups, Dora backpacks and Dora plush dolls. Each year, there is a new spin— Dora the princess, Dora the homemaker—to reinvigorate the line. These products are nominally reviewed with the show's creators. Occasionally, product designers are constrained based on the educational and developmental aims of the show, but such limits are rare. The changes a show can go through on the way to the toy store are also evident in the Dora princess line—the icon of self-empowerment and female problem-solving transformed into Rapunzel. For Brodsky, though, the mandate is clear: "Every year we have to keep reinventing her."

In the conference room on the forty-fourth floor, the ratio of publicist to journalist was about 8 to 1. It was not the most easy-going setting. As Manhattan shivered in twenty-degree sunshine five hundred feet below the room's wall of windows, the phalanx showed me around a set of tables where merchandise was arrayed in a sneak preview of Nickelodeon's offerings at Toy Fair. "Look, but don't touch!" admonished one of the junior publicists. I couldn't tell whether he was kidding.

First up was the Let's Get Ready Vanity, which features a Dora doll with a longer haircut that is ideal for kids to style. A map holder with replaceable cards and bilingual phrases uttered at the touch of a button were some of the reasons the set carried a suggested retail price of $79.99. The phalanx told me that this play set is classified as a role-playing toy—one of the hottest categories going. It follows previous years' Dora kitchen and cash register. Even pricier, at $99.99, is the Bouncing Pony Arcade Ride, with patent-pending technology that prevents any fingers or toes from getting squeezed by the springs underneath. It also talks—as do most toys these days. "It's like having an arcade ride at home!" enthused one publicist, redundantly.

What's striking about these latest *Dora* products, and many others on display at Toy Fair, is how remote they can get from the well-intentioned efforts of the creators of the original show, who spent years refining its curriculum and believed wholeheartedly in its beneficial effects on kids' self esteem and intellectual development. The same consultants who handled the show's bilingual curriculum and ensured that the scripts hit all the points of Howard Gardner's multiple-intelligences theory were not sampling the wares at Toy Fair or driving decisions about the toy strategy. In fact, it has long worked the opposite way, with toy concepts shaping children's entertainment.

Although Dora has years of backstory and a well-established character, Brodsky's challenge has been to make her appeal as broad as possible. In the early days it was not clear whether a wide swath of American consumers would embrace a Latina girl. "She has been an adventure," Brodsky said. "When she was first introduced, we didn't know how deep it would go. People have really made an emotional connection. She's aspirational, but you also want to be her friend." I asked whether she is effectively making Dora evolve as a character by creating new product lines for her year after year. "She remains such an iconic character that her qualities have to shine through," she said. "So when we created the fairytale princess line, she was saving Boots. She wasn't just going to be a damsel in distress."

Brodsky and her department had already begun developing prototypes for *Ni Hao*. But there would be no final decision about whether products would be released until the show appeared on the air. The wait-and-see attitude in preschool TV stands in marked contrast to the protocol with feature films. The same 2–5 target audience for *Ni Hao* was able to buy a *Ratatouille* plush doll the same day the Disney cartoon arrived in theaters.

I thought about my daughter, how she was now too old and tall to scoot around our living room on the Dora's Fairytale Adventure Activity Ride-On—essentially a stool with four plastic wheels that toddlers propel with their feet. Who knew how much longer she'd even be enamored with Dora? Yet the products will continue. The last items I saw on my tour were snowboards, skis, and helmets decorated with Dora and *SpongeBob SquarePants* images. They were already being sold in a handful of resort ski shops. But the real masterstroke was a three-year phase-in that will make the branded goods the official rental equipment in all eight mountains run by American Skiing Company, including Killington, the Canyons, and Steamboat. In 2010, it isn't clear what the Dora TV show will look like, but the character will live on. And as Mickey Mouse, Transformers, and countless other toy brands have shown, nostalgia can usher in a whole new wave of business down the line.

One inescapable phenomenon at Toy Fair is the melding of traditional toy companies and traditional entertainment entities. Everyone, in a sense, is trying to solve the same puzzle of how to engage preschoolers. This new reality is evident upon a visit to the Toy Fair exhibition space of Hasbro, the multibillion-dollar company behind items such as Tonka trucks, Play-Doh, and *Star Wars* action figures. One of Hasbro's lines is Playskool, which specializes in baby and preschool toys. Just in time for Toy Fair, the company had introduced a line of products under the umbrella Made for Me—basic nursery items now endowed with an MP3 player capable of storing two hours of digital audio. The Made for Me play mat, for example, has a player with oversize buttons that a baby can learn to push while in repose. It may be called Made for Me, but it seemed abundantly clear that this innovation, like so much in the baby-preschool entertainment world, is principally made for parents. I asked one of the models on hand to demonstrate products whom she thought the MP3 player was for. "It's great because this way parents don't have to listen to the same nursery rhyme over and over and over," she responded.

Most of the wares at the Javits Center were not intended to make parents' lives easier (not directly, anyway). Rather, their purpose was pure entertainment, a goal increasingly at odds with the educational bent of preschool TV shows. The dynamic is far different in other countries. In Britain, for example, which has a long history of children's TV, the goal is explicitly entertainment and there is none of the pretense of education that characterizes American preschool shows. Greg Lynn, the executive producer of a British show called *Fifi and the Flowertots,* told the *Wall Street Journal* that he has to generate $3.6 million in merchandise retail sales to fund ten minutes of the show. That reality helps explain why characters in the series include a rabbit and a pet caterpillar—both of which make for appealing plush toys. Gary Pope, a London-based children's marketing consultant, puts it more bluntly. "Children's television shows are just giant toy ads," he said. In the United Kingdom, that dynamic has only gotten more pronounced since a government ban on junk food ads aimed at kids under sixteen, intended to curb obesity, has put the financial squeeze on many top producers. ITV, for example, decided to stop producing new preschool shows because it cannot recover the junk food ad revenue elsewhere.

Technology, the biggest weapon in the counterattack against the junk food ad police, fills every corner of Toy Fair. At Mattel's showroom, the company's Fisher-Price brand, the largest infant and preschool company in terms of sales, introduced a $99.99 item called the Smart Cycle. Aimed at kids from three to six years old, it is a stationary bicycle with a video monitor attached. Only by pedaling the bike can kids play the games. A press release said the cycle was part of Richard Simmons's "personal crusade" to fight childhood obesity. Fisher-Price, which produces many of Sesame Workshop's popular toys, also displayed a specially designed MP3 player and digital camera for kids as young as three, which it planned to start selling for Christmas 2007. KGOY indeed. Revenues in the "learning and exploration" category have soared 25 percent since 2003, to about $400 million. "It's not too young to start thinking about college at age four," reasoned Anita Frazier, a toy analyst with consumer research firm NPD Group, presumably with a straight face.

At Toy Fair, like its summer cousin the Licensing Show, one grasps the scope of the tie-in product universe, from blow-up superhero suits to prewashed spinach leaves. Long-established brands dominate, but the upstarts sometimes leave an impression with old-fashioned showmanship. In 2006, a regional public-TV fixture called The Big Comfy Couch installed an actual couch inside a faux living room where they hawked the show. A series called Toot & Puddle had two people dressed in pig costumes shaking hands. McDonald's erected a bright yellow hut in which to plug its line of preschool DVDs called, yes, McKids.

For brand-new shows, the merchandising windup happens in

stages. First they spread the word to manufacturers and retailers about what the show is, to whom it appeals, and why the merchandise theoretically will fly off the shelves. Then they introduce a small collection of products and gradually widen the selection over a few months as the public generates interest. With a monster hit such as *Dora*, the process can extend over several years. The rollout is more protracted than a mainstream animated movie, for example, most of whose products are in stores a couple of months before the film gets released. In many cases, the release of toys happens gradually—first with an exclusive deal with a certain chain and then broader deals with big-box retailers. "You don't want to have all your stuff in Kmart or Target and then realize the show isn't meeting expectations," one veteran toy executive explained.

Ni Hao, Kai-lan producer Mary Harrington showed me some prototypes during my visit to the Burbank studio and told me that when merchandise executives were shown early artwork from the show, "They flipped over it." Merchandise can quickly net billions, Nickelodeon has learned, but it also can serve as an even more potent gateway to a family's loyalty, which is a renewable source of revenue. A TV show lasts only a half hour, whereas toys and clothes and backpacks and the like fully immerse households in the show's characters. When Tom Freston, the CEO of Nickelodeon parent Viacom who was ousted in 2006, toured the Burbank studio, he stopped in Harrington's office and noticed the *Ni Hao* drawings and sample figurines. "China is everything," he told her portentously. He nodded slowly, studying the characters before adding, "These look great."

For all the success Nickelodeon has had in the ratings and as a kid-oriented business over the past generation, it is interesting to note that it has really only ever had four "home run" shows in terms of licensing, and two in the preschool arena: *Blue's Clues* and *Dora*. *Hey Arnold!*, for example, was a hit on the air but a dud in stores. In the words of Nickelodeon Preschool president Brown Johnson, "What you want to watch and what you want to wear are not necessarily the same thing." New entrants often succeed by targeting their programs at specific niches and merchandising accordingly. Often, that means strict lines are drawn between the sexes—*Bob the Builder* Legos for boys, pink *Angelina the Ballerina* purses for girls. "With a boys' show, you're going to have bad guys and good guys. You're going to have all the things that drive little boys," said Al Kahn, chairman and CEO of 4Kids, which controls the Bratz and Teenage Mutant Ninja Turtles. "If you're doing a girls show, you're going to have fashion. They want to be rich and famous or they want to be a mom—take their pick."

Feeling dispirited by the breakneck race to seed brand loyalties from the womb, I was glad to stumble on a booth displaying the wares of an Israeli company called Edushape. An offshoot of a plastics manufacturer founded in 1957, it makes toys mainly for the infant and preschool market. Few if any of their toys require batteries or assembly. They are basic blocks, balls—what child development experts call "manipulatives," physical objects designed to cultivate their senses of sight and touch and to develop muscles and coordination. I struck up a conversation with Judith Culberson, the company's national sales manager, and told her about what brought me to Toy Fair. "Our new line has the theme, Bonding With Babies, and we're trying to do everything but the electronic world," she said. "We still like the fact that kids are going to use their brains to figure things out."

I talked to her about my daughter, Margot, about Margot's brother-to-be, and about the battleground that is the contemporary American living room. As a parent, she understood, but she also held her ground. She told me about a woman who visited Edushape's booth at the ABC Kids Expo in Las Vegas—an event similar to Toy Fair but more expressly geared toward babies and preschoolers. "She was pushing a stroller and her daughter could not have been three years old," she said. "I looked down and saw that her daughter was wearing headphones and watching a portable DVD player. Completely plugged in." The girl asked for a new DVD and, in one motion, the woman flipped through a stack and replaced the one that was already in the player. "She turned to me and asked, 'Does that make me a bad mom?' I wasn't going to say so because she was a customer, but I was horrified. I just found an excuse to walk away."

I asked if Edushape was feeling any pressure, especially given the electronic offerings I had seen elsewhere at Toy Fair, to move in that direction to keep the company financially strong. On the contrary, she said. "We're trying to tell people to take a step back. Children need to have some engagement. Parents now expect somebody else to do that. They're trying to get the school to do it or grandma to do it, but the parent needs to take the time. Otherwise, what kind of people are we raising? Are we raising them to expect the world to come to them predigested? Children learn by example. They learn from what you put out there for them. And what do they learn if they're wearing headphones or just sitting on the couch?"

That sentiment returned me to the guilty realm of a parent who had modeled watching TV for his child. Was I basically teaching her how to sit on the couch, developing in her a talent for TV watcher? Definitive answers were still hard to come by, and my trip to Toy Fair had hardly reassured me about the notion of corporate interests luring my daughter and, worse, me. To help put my disorienting travels through the Javits Center in context, I decided to seek out one person whom I had wanted to meet since my quest began, Julie Clark, the creator of Baby Einstein. A person defined by her experience at Toy Fair whose entire identity and fortune were bound up in the idea of kids learning while on the couch, Clark never seemed to apologize for it. In fact, the name and packaging suggested babies could do more than just learn on the couch. They could become cultured. I made plans to fly to Colorado to visit Julie Clark. Judith Culberson, the saleswoman for Edushape, had posed the rhetorical question "What kind of children are we raising?" The answer at this moment in civilization, given the enormous sales of the videos, like it or not, is Baby Einstein children. I was determined to find out what exactly that meant.

8

ZERO HOUR

Birth of the Postpartum Demographic

O n the three hundred days a year when the sun shines on Centennial, Colorado, the Rocky Mountains appear to rise directly from Julie Clark's backyard. Their snowy peaks fill the rear windows of her sprawling, sunlit mansion, which sits on a bluff on Flanders Street, one of several streets with incongruous European names in a subdivision called Chaparral just southeast of Denver. Aside from its spectacular mountain scenery, Centennial is a quintessentially late-model American community, with clusters of oversize, off-white homes occupying a constellation of cul-de-sacs with no sidewalks. The streets all funnel down to an access road that spills out onto a bigger thoroughfare lined with big-box stores and shopping malls. One, the Arapahoe Center, has a movie theater called the Chinese that is a scale replica of Mann's Chinese Theatre, the temple of cinema in Hollywood where stars from Charlie Chaplin to Johnny Depp have left their handprints.

Little of the development around Clark's house existed a decade ago. Centennial was incorporated in 2000, with a population of 103,000 that is 87 percent white. But history, census data, urban planning—none of it matters much once you step inside the Clarks' sanctum sanctorum. Its amenities are a fantasy straight out of a high-gloss real estate brochure: skylights, vaulted ceilings, professional-grade kitchen appliances, multiple guest bedrooms, landscaping emphasizing native species. A sound system sends tasteful music through unobtrusively mounted speakers, the volume modulated to allow for the sound of the wind chimes just outside the door.

These are the fruits of success, evidently, when you have created a paradigm shift that is still reverberating through American business and culture. Clark achieved that by joining two deceptively simple words that explode when put together: Baby Einstein. With some assistance from her husband, Bill, and a borrowed video camera, she created the line of infant videos, targeting children from three to thirty-six months, which first arrived in stores in 1997. After building the company to a level of $25 million in annual sales just five years later, she and Bill sold it to Disney for a sum reported to be at least that high. She hasn't had to work since. Clark earned a place in history for her game-changing invention, but she isn't a figure in children's entertainment in the mode of Fred Rogers or Anne Wood or Joan Ganz Cooney, working well into her autumn years. Instead, she cashed out big after a few intense years of work and, though she recently returned to teaching and being a mother to two girls now ten and thirteen, she is essentially on the sidelines.

It is difficult to overstate the importance of Baby Einstein as a business and cultural force, both then and now. When it first hit store shelves, no entertainment company had thought to address in a concerted way viewers under the age of two. Today it is a brand valued at $1 billion controlled by Disney, as well as the opener of the latest Pandora's box in children's media. Two cable TV channels aimed at babies and toddlers from three to thirty-six months—BabyFirstTV and BabyTV—have launched in the wake of Baby Einstein, not to mention a raft of video imitators such as Baby Genius, Baby Prodigy, Curious Buddies, Sesame Beginnings, and Eebee. Many have tried and failed to cut into Baby Einstein's 80-plus percent market share. Across the larger business landscape there is now a sense that the old reservations about marketing to babies have largely evaporated.

When Clark invited me to spend a couple of hours in her house, I had to begin with one question that had been on my mind since not long after my daughter was born: Where did the idea for Baby Einstein come from?

"The only video I knew was called *Baby Mugs*," she said. "That was a woman in California who videotaped a bunch of faces from her baby's playgroup because babies like looking at babies. And she sold it, but it wasn't particularly successful. Baby Einstein was certainly pretty remedial as far as the entertainment. This was done by me, in my basement, with no video experience. It wasn't what you'd call slick. But hers was extremely rudimentary. And it didn't do particularly well. But I knew that it existed, so I knew that something else was out there but my child didn't really like it."

Befitting the Sunday morning hour, Clark was dressed casually—white pants and a navy cotton long-sleeve shirt. Her toenails were painted a glossy red. Her skin was tan, her teeth a vibrant white. The speakers played a tune by pop electronica group

Thievery Corporation. She curled her hands around a large mug containing cappuccino, looking out toward the mountains for a moment to reconnect with the origins of Baby Einstein.

"So I thought, well, OK, that's not what I wanted anyway, a bunch of baby faces," she said. "I wanted something that was going to expose my daughter to stuff that I loved, having taught art and literature. So it was, for me, a completely empty field. And it didn't make sense to me that what I was looking for didn't exist. I wasn't trying to make videos for babies as much as I was trying to make a really interactive experience for babies that was a lot like a board book. So I coined this whole term 'video board book' because you sat with your baby and looked at books that were basically a bunch of pictures. . . . That was a great way to interact with your child. But I thought, Why couldn't you do that on a video screen so my baby's not going to eat the book? She's actually going to watch and she can sit on my lap and we can dance and move arms and do all this fun stuff."

As Alice wonders in Lewis Carroll's *Alice in Wonderland,* "And what is the use of a book without pictures and conversations?" What amazed me was that Clark, unlike almost everyone I had encountered in the world of baby and toddler entertainment, had not convened focus groups, studied research papers, or conducted tests of any kind before making her videos.

"Parents responded to that," she said, "because they felt this isn't a big, powerhouse room of executives sitting around a room trying to figure out what babies are going to look at and like. This is just a mom who spends time with her baby and knows what babies want to see. And the truth is, babies responded to it because I did have a sense of what babies like, but it was only innate because I had a baby."

An English major at Michigan State with no formal psychology or child development training, Clark taught high school in East Detroit right after college. She was twenty-two. "I taught a lot of kids who, through no fault of theirs, had families who didn't care or they had a single mom who was working all day," Clark said. "You go in and you look like one of the kids. You've learned all this stuff about education but then you walk into the classroom and you realize you don't know anything about education." After four years of teaching, Clark took a job at a company called Optical Data, which put educational materials on laser discs and marketed them to schools. Her husband, Bill, also worked at Optical Data. They first met at a company meeting in New Jersey.

In 1997, at the age of thirty-two, the then-new mother teamed with her husband, who had just sold a child-oriented science company to Cox Communications, to produce the first *Baby Einstein* video, which cost eighteen thousand dollars of the couple's savings. They shot it in the basement of their home in Alpharetta, Georgia, with borrowed video equipment. Capturing the experience of watching a *Baby Einstein* video is difficult to do in words. Against a black backdrop, baby toys move through the frame, sometimes for a few seconds, sometimes for just a moment. Often, classical music plays. Depending on the video, you might glimpse a Braque painting or a pride of lions. It's a fast-moving pastiche of two- and three-dimensional objects.

At the time, Clark's only research consisted of reading an article in *Newsweek*. "It was called 'Your Child's Brain,'" she recalled. "It was this really excellent article that took all of this research out of the gobbledy-gook of the scientific terminology and just made it accessible to someone like me, who didn't have a science background and who was a mom. It took all of this information, like the fact that babies see black and white more clearly than they do light pink or light blue, which is funny, because that's what we put in their nursery. But they actually see red, black, and white a lot more. I was reading it because I had a baby and I was interested."

One reason Clark believed the video board book concept was viable was the fact that she had grown up watching "a lot of TV when I was a kid. I was an only child. I watched a lot with my mom and dad—*Happy Days, Laverne & Shirley, Love Boat, Gilligan's Island,* all that schlocky stuff. But when you look back at it now it's all so harmless and sweet compared to the garbage that's on TV now. *H.R. Pufnstuf, Sesame Street* was even so different then. Mister Rogers. I don't think he was Mister Child Development Expert either, but he was just this quiet, gentlemanly, fatherly, or grandfatherly figure that you just liked as a child. It was the simplicity. There wasn't that noise."

Clark is an easygoing person who starts a lot of her sentences with "And you know, the truth is . . ." In the flat vowel sounds of her native Michigan, she utters no oaths stronger than "crap" or "garbage." When she talks about banning the "s-word" in her home, it's *stupid,* not the one you assume. She clearly had no idea that her modest basement invention would make her a lightning rod and that in itself gives her an endearing quality. Because her husband has made donations to Republican campaigns, she was seated in the First Lady's box during President Bush's 2007 State of the Union address. That prompted an attack by Jacob Weisberg of Slate.com. He called the videos a "scam" in a piece headlined "Bush's *Baby Einstein* Gaffe: The President Lionizes a Mountebank." At the center of Weisberg's rant, as with many critiques of baby videos, is the American Academy of Pediatrics recommendation, which most of its members do not follow, and which 6 percent of parents have ever heard of.

Critics of the videos got fresh ammunition in August 2007, when the *Journal of Pediatrics* published a study by Frederick Zimmerman, Dimitri Christakis, and Andrew Meltzoff of the University of Washington. The pediatricians are longtime critics of television, and authored the 2004 study that landed on the front page of the *New York Times* by asserting that attention disorders were closely associated with heavy TV viewing. In the '07 study, they looked at children under two whose parents reported regular viewing of videos and television. One of the conclusions that generated headlines: regular exposure to an hour of baby videos a day, especially among children ages eight to sixteen months, resulted in them understanding six to eight fewer vocabulary words. Reading or telling stories to those same kids who also watched media was found to add just two to three words.

Clark posted a response on her Web site. "I read the press release from the University of Washington and was shaken," it began. "Harming babies? With Mozart?" She went on to contend that the study was flawed in many respects: by using telephone methodology and therefore ignoring the environment in the home; by obscuring the fact that the average child watched videos for just eight minutes a day; and by suggesting that the intent of *Baby Einstein* was to serve as a babysitter.

The knottiest issue with baby videos, *Einstein* or otherwise, is that research on babies' reactions to TV is not easy, for several reasons, among them the validity of responses from preverbal subjects. Rachel Barr at Georgetown is one of the leading researchers of media's effects on infants. Her Early Learning Project, by continually recruiting volunteer parents and infants, has made several noteworthy discoveries in recent years. Working with a team of thirty undergraduate and graduate students, Barr established a game that would be used on a research subject. It involves a hand puppet with a mitten and a bell inside. When the mitten is removed, the bell can be rung. Researchers remove the mitten and ring the bell in front of the infant and then return twenty-four hours later to see if the baby emulates the action by removing and shaking the mitten. One study determined that infants six months old were able to emulate the action equally well after a video demonstration or a live demonstration. At twelve months, babies needed the video demonstration repeated in order to respond in the same way they did to the live demonstration.

While certain studies have suggested links between TV and video exposure and problems with sleep, cognitive development, and behavior, there is no definitive proof. Neither is there definitive scientific evidence that any baby video can enhance a child's development, as many videos claim. Critics of Baby Einstein insist the DVDs are training a generation to become TV viewers at an earlier age than ever, while also failing to fulfill their marketing promises. One activist group, Campaign for a Commercial-Free Childhood, filed a complaint with the Federal Trade Commission that was still pending in mid-2007. Michael Rich, the pediatrician who runs the Center on Media and Child Health in Boston, said his daily review of the latest studies confirms there is "no evidence whatsoever that this does any good."

Along with Baby Einstein, one of the targets of the FTC complaint was Sesame Workshop, which elicited an angry response from many quarters in 2006 by releasing a line of baby videos called *Sesame Beginnings*. The videos introduced baby versions of familiar *Sesame Street* characters—Big Bird, Elmo, Cookie Monster. They wore diapers and had smaller faces, and they were in the care of a parent, grandparent, or guardian in every scene. The muppet scenes were combined with live-action scenes showing parents interacting with their babies.

Nearly four decades of fond loyalty and esteem for the Sesame characters created a boomerang effect in the media reaction. This wasn't just any set of baby videos—these were internationally treasured characters being perverted for a cravenly commercial goal, critics charged. Even ostensibly objective news anchors such as NPR's Steve Inskeep and the CBS *Early Show*'s Harry Smith voiced skepticism about the DVDs (as they have about Baby Einstein), asserting that *Sesame Beginnings* was a transparent marketing ploy, an attempt to steal market share away from Baby Einstein in a dicey new market segment in which Big Bird and Elmo had no business being. Sales have been sluggish, and Sesame's plans to make any more *Beginnings* DVDs are in limbo. The organization believed then and maintains now that most people missed the point. They felt that modeling parent behavior was a better bet than trying to dazzle a baby with quick cuts and a Mozart violin quartet.

Rosemarie Truglio, the level-headed research chief for Sesame, not only endorsed the videos based on her child development training at Columbia University, but actually appeared in the videos with her son. She said the venture was worthwhile. "We went out on a limb," Truglio said a year after the launch. "There are a lot of infant development people who are wary of *Baby Einstein* because it's moving too fast with too many cuts to really model parent-child interaction." In the spring of 2006, when the line of DVDs debuted with a baby-shower-themed event for stroller-pushing parents at New York's DGA Theater, I asked Truglio why it was better for babies and their parents to view a video showing a child and parent rolling a ball to each other instead of turning the TV off and actually rolling the ball in real life. She said the research was clear that many parents, burdened by job duties or their single-parent status, lack basic parenting skills. "We have had contact with a lot of parents who didn't even know that they needed to get down on the floor and play with their child," she said. When I mentioned that to Michael Rich in Boston, he said, "OK, so why are there babies and muppets in the video at all? Why not market it just for parents instead of putting the Sesame characters on there?" It's a question with which a lot of figures in baby and preschool entertainment had been grappling. Baby-FirstTV started off with several hours of programming aimed at parents but had to pare back significantly when they realized how unpopular it was with parents.

Sales may not be strong for *Sesame Beginnings,* but Truglio finally got a bit of support in the spring of 2007, when University of Massachusetts psychology professor Dan Anderson, the veteran researcher known for his role in shaping *Blue's Clues,* presented early results of an ongoing study of *Sesame Beginnings.* At the biennial meeting of the Society for Research in Child Development, Anderson and his colleagues said parents who had viewed the videos for two weeks interacted more with their kids when the TV was off. They conceded, however, that data from a control group—i.e., families who did not watch the video—were still being collected.

The baby segment, in a way, was what sparked my interest in writing this book. At the same time Margot began watching bits of *Sesame Street* on those early, early mornings, she also got into a series of Nickelodeon DVDs branded for babies under the banner *Curious Buddies.* I responded to the softness of the packaging and the title. I had loved the *Curious George* books when I was a child, and, like a lot of parents, I relish the idea of my child being curious about the world around her. Between the ages of one and two, Margot wore out three *Curious Buddies* DVDs, especially one called *Let's Play!,* a cheaply produced montage of live-action scenes of kids in the park, doing Ring around the Rosie and sing-ing "Heads, Shoulders, Knees, and Toes," combined with puppet sequences done by the same company that produces *Jack's Big Music Show* for Nickelodeon. Watching Margot become mesmer-ized by these videos was my first introduction to the power of baby and toddler entertainment.

Teletubbies proved equally revolutionary from the moment it appeared on American airwaves in 1998, having been a ringing success in its native Britain a year before. Widely acknowledged to be the first show whose stated aim—rather than accidental feat—was appealing to children under three, the dreamlike show features four alien creatures with antennae and TV screens embedded in their bellies, because, creator Anne Wood told me, "that's where children feel things, in the stomach." (It's a new definition of the 1950s condition "TV tummy.") They speak in a giggly stream of semi-intelligible not-quite words—sounds that little viewers enjoy but critics attack as retarding speech and literacy. Producers and PBS responded that, in keeping with child development research, they were simply trying to create an environment in which babies and toddlers could emulate the straightforward, positive action on-screen: Teletubbies playing with butterflies and giant balls in a bright green meadow under a smiling sun. "The brilliance of the show is that the camera never moves," says Dan Gurlitz of Koch Entertainment, who distributes a newer show by the makers of *Teletubbies* called *Brum*. As opposed to, say, *Dora the Explorer,* which typically has about 140 cuts per twenty-four-minute episode (in turn about one-third of an average prime-time episode geared toward adults), "the steadiness is definitely the design. At a year old, babies are able to discern patterns, color, and music. Their favorite game is peekaboo. So *Teletubbies* simulates peekaboo by never changing the angle or cutting away."

Clark didn't make fancy sets or order specialized props when she set about making her *Baby Einstein* videos. She used the same toys that she was using the rest of the time she was entertaining her children in real life. Many of the toys are preserved in her office, which has vaulted ceilings and ten-foot windows. Bookshelves line two walls, floor to ceiling. They hold everything from novels (*One Hundred Years of Solitude*) to current events (Bill Maher's *New Rules*) to baby/child books. Mixed in with the regular books are Baby Einstein books, videos, memorabilia, and some of the puppets and toys used in making the videos. There is a framed picture of Clark with Oprah Winfrey and awards and plaques and, on another shelf, the red hat she wore to kindergarten in Germany.

Her survey of the shelves conjured a few memories, but since her five-year consulting deal with Disney ended in 2006, she has become more jaundiced about the ways Disney distorted her original concept. She said the company has spurned her ideas and taken the company in a much lower-brow direction typified by their decision to make the DVD *Baby MacDonald: A Day on the Farm* instead of a title Clark had proposed, *Baby Lewis & Clark*.

The main trait that emerged from two hours of conversation is purposeful idealism. Clark started her company in her basement, on a shoestring, for the simple reason that babies needed exposure to art and would naturally be engaged. That's it—no consultants, no panel of experts, no focus groups or seals of approval from parenting groups. She just went out and did it and had no idea how it would be received by the larger public. She didn't fret or wring her hands or read scientific studies. And that's the foundation on which she continues to stand. She considers herself first and foremost a mom.

"I just kept that idea in my mind of a video board book,"

she said. "I just thought, OK, this is going to be simple images. I wanted it to be like page turns on the screen, from image to image, as if I was sitting reading a book with my child. So I had that basic premise in my head, and in terms of the images, I just knew what my child liked looking at. I thought, Oh, she likes looking at this black-and-white spotted cow, so I'm going to put that in the video. Or, she likes looking at our cat, so I'm going to put our cat up on the tabletop and see if I can get her to keep still for ten seconds. So it was really very basic. And then I edited it using Adobe Premiere on our home computer, with no editing experience at all."

Clark shot all of the raw footage for the videos at night when her daughter, Aspen, was sleeping, or during her naptimes. "It was funny because I didn't know how to operate any of this equipment. I had these big strobe lights that my friend had given me so I could get good light in my basement. They were so delicate, if you just bumped it, they'd go 'poof' and you'd go, 'Oh, shoot, there goes my shoot for the night.' I didn't have all the equipment to go get a new bulb or a crew who could deal with it. But that was really the fun part about Baby Einstein, even after we had tremendous success and started selling a lot of product. I was still the person running the hobby lobby because I thought, Oh, I have to put sunglasses on this puppet! It'd be so cute to, like, get little sunglasses for this puppet. It was so organic about how I was pulling ideas together. It was just what makes sense to me and what does my baby like. And the premise was that if my baby liked it, other babies were going to like it because babies are babies."

Preparation for a shoot basically consisted of Clark sticking her hand in a puppet and playing pretend. The concept was so potent that even the puppets themselves become minor deities. "Everyone knows Bard, the one who goes 'blaaahh' on *Baby Ein-*

stein. Response to the first puppet was so great. Everyone said, 'My baby loves that!' So the next video that I made after *Baby Bach* was *Baby Shakespeare* and I thought, Oh, I'm going to use that puppet extensively. He'll be the Bard. I contacted this woman who had the company that made this puppet. She was in North Dakota and she worked in a factory of Native Americans and they were bath mitts for the most part. I called her up and asked if she would make some puppets that I could use in the videos and she said, 'That's great.' Then, when I was making *Baby Van Gogh*, I thought, 'Oh, this will be perfect. I can have a goat and call it Baby Van Goat.' So I called her up and asked her to make a goat puppet in blue and gold. It was this tiny company but she sold twenty thousand a year. Bard became an item at The Right Start, a bath puppet." Upon the sale to Disney, the North Dakota manufacturer made more than $1 million.

"In the beginning, I didn't even think about it," Clark said. "Then people said, 'I'd love it if you'd put my toys in your video.' But I never did a deal where I said, 'I'm going to put all Barbie stuff in this video.' It was always stuff that I loved and that my baby loved."

The let's-put-on-a-show attitude of Baby Einstein disappeared soon after it was subsumed into a company of Disney's scope, Clark said. "The most difficult part about having sold Baby Einstein is seeing what it's become. To me, that whole feeling, that whole organic nature of it is completely gone, and I knew it would be." In place of the art and music and cultural exposure that Clark has always maintained was the core of the videos, Disney has gone mass retail. Consumers who would buy the videos at Wal-Mart, as opposed to a boutique such as The Right Start, where Clark first got traction, are more motivated by a video showing farm animals than one showing more exotic creatures.

I had to ask Clark what her perspective was on the other side of the living room transaction. How did she think her customers were using the videos and did she ever think of the child development ramifications?

"They say they [watch it with their baby] because it sounds really good. But I don't know if it's used that way," she said. "The truth is, probably when I was making the videos a lot of people were putting their baby down in front of them and then going to take a shower, which is the reality of being a stay-at-home mom. It's four o'clock and you think, I haven't showered all day and I've got to make a phone call. So that's kind of the reality of it. But I really was of the bent that this could be so cool and interactive and it could give parents who might never expose their child to Mozart—parents who themselves have never heard Bach or Beethoven might give them the opportunity to listen and expose their child to something that isn't part of their natural daily life."

The consensus among people working in the preschool industry had been that the name Baby Einstein alone, far more than the content of the videos, was Clark's true masterstroke. I asked her how the name came to be.

"I wish there was an awesome story, but here's the deal: I sat down at the kitchen table. We were in the midst of making the video and I was thinking, God, what am I going to call this? I didn't even anticipate having a company, I just had this one video. And I thought, Oh, what about 'Baby Einstein?' It was very funny because at the time I said that to my husband and he was so appalled, he was a physics major. He's like, 'You can't call it "Baby Einstein"! That's, like, *Einstein*. You can't degrade Einstein's name.' And I'm like, no, it's perfect, it says exactly what it is. It's for babies, and Einstein was, like, this amazing person who, you know, we all kind of think, Wouldn't it be cool to have our child have the kind of intelligence Einstein had? He was an amazing violinist, loved classical music, loved art. He kind of encompassed all these things. He was a little wacky, too, and came from this weird dyslexic background and was able to change his life around and do these amazing things. To me, thinking outside the box, that name just encompassed all that. So once I had the name I just got out my daughter's crayons and drew that little head and the logo that's on everything still, and that's pretty exciting."

Clark never thought twice about the potential copyright issues or how the Albert Einstein estate would feel about it. After about a year of selling the videos, Clark said, a letter arrived from an attorney representing Hebrew University of Jerusalem, the institution to which Einstein left his papers. The letter came at a tender moment in the life of the young company. The first year of sales totaled $100,000. The second year was headed to $1 million, and still there were only two full-time employees, Clark and her husband. Clark said she was "immediately horrified" by the possibility of a lawsuit taking the name away and she and her husband decided the name was vital. "We filed a suit against them first, for threatening our business," Clark said. "Then they countersued and that's when things got ugly. We had to get lawyers involved and get into all this stuff I never knew anything about because I was a teacher. Anyway, we pushed back and said, look, Einstein in our minds is synonymous with smart. You can open up Webster's dictionary and see two definitions for *Einstein*. One is the physicist and one is a highly intelligent person. If you came to me and said, 'My daughter is an Einstein,' I wouldn't think she was related to Einstein. I'd think she was a really smart kid. So we pushed back and got into this lawsuit issue with them and ultimately did settle. We paid them a lot of money but it was worth it to us because we saw this tremendous growth and success. We felt we had this really excellent brand that was really becoming recognized. And I didn't want to call it anything else. I didn't want to call it 'Baby Genius,' that was wrong. 'Brainy Babies' was wrong. 'Baby Prodigy' was wrong. It was 'Baby Einstein.'"

The U.S. Patent Office recognized that Baby Einstein had established the right to brand something, as Clark put it, "Baby plus historical figure," for example, Picasso or Galileo. "I learned that you want someone who's been dead for more than seventy-five years because then they couldn't come back and sue you," she said. "So you wouldn't do a 'Baby Goodall' because Jane Goodall is still alive and it'd be a big lawsuit. So that broad trademark ability was excellent because then when Brainy Baby wanted to put out something similar, they said no because people will think that's Baby Einstein."

Another one of the astounding facts of Baby Einstein's rise: it attained its prominence without a single advertisement. "It was all word of mouth," Clark said. "Starting with a specialty retailer was a great idea. To be honest, I didn't know anything about business. I didn't know how to get into Wal-Mart or any of those stores. I just went to the store where I bought things for my daughter, which was Right Start."

Clark said she has often been struck by the inescapable fact that she was only able to produce Baby Einstein because she did not know what she was doing.

"People in the entertainment industry would watch these videos and say, 'Oh, my God, I never could have made this because it's so simple,'" she said. "And that's why it was successful. That's why babies liked it. People in entertainment just can't think that way. They think, 'It has to be slick and I have to have loud music.' *Baby Einstein* was just about, if you can try to see the world through the eyes of a baby, how awesome is that?! I remember taking Aspen to the beach and putting her in the sand. She just stood there. It was like trying to think of what that must have been like for a baby to be there in the sand and feel it under their toes. Surrounded by this expanse of crashing water. That experience is so pure and amazing and we don't even see it. Give a baby a flower and they're just like"—her eyes widened in an awestruck expression—"it's so cool. You don't have to give a baby all of the noise. You just don't have to do it."

I asked her about the common quip that the magnetic power of Baby Einstein is such that parents have nicknamed it 'Baby Crack.' She smiled and shrugged. "When you think about, what are board books like?" she said. "You read a board book over and over and you want to pull your eye out. But it's so simple. Look at *Goodnight Moon*. It's so simple and such a classic. If we could just try to get back to that."

She doesn't accept any responsibility for feeding into parents' impulse to pressure kids to succeed from birth.

"There are always going to be parents who pressure their kids. My kids couldn't be less pressured. So there are going to be parents who buy Baby Einstein because they think it's going to make their kid smarter. But then there's a ton of other people who think, This is just good stuff. I know my kid is going to be exposed to TV, so I have a choice. I can turn on the Disney Channel or I can put in a *Baby Einstein* video and if I put in a *Baby Einstein* video, I know what I'm getting. There are no commercials. There's not a lot of noise. There is content that's appropriate to my child. You're always going to have people, that other side, who say, 'It's hothousing kids, it's forcing kids.' And the thing is, babies love it. I wasn't making kids watch it. I didn't strap them to a chair. It's not like *Clockwork Orange*."

I didn't have to ask any more questions. Clark was officially on a roll.

"People will say, 'How can you call it that? Baby Einstein implies it's going to make them smart.' But you know what? It's a great name. Here's the answer: it's a great name. It told you what it was. It's about stimulating babies. It's not about educating babies. It's about stimulating them in ways that they might not have been. People can say all the negative things they want about TV, but I think TV can be a great way to take your kids on a field trip to a place they might never get to. We may never go to Antarctica, but I can pop a tape in with my kids and see *March of the Penguins* and watch these penguins do things I might never see in my lifetime. Can a book do that? Sure. Is a book great? Absolutely. Why not do both? Why not give your kids the experience of hearing the music and seeing the motion and then they can go to the library and check out a book about it? In moderation, everything is OK. As long as the content is good, I have no problem with TV. I watched a ton of TV and I read a lot. People need to calm down. Why can't you just ever be in the middle? This is a weird topic to talk about, but it's like why do you have to be pro-choice or pro-life? Why can't you be somewhere in the middle and kind of accept it but believe that it's wrong. Everything is OK in moderation if it's good content."

In Clark's view, society has much bigger fish to fry than whether junior is watching a few minutes of a *Baby Einstein* video while Mom makes a phone call. "Forty percent of kids born to women in their twenties are born out of wedlock," she said, her mouth falling open. "I saw this movie, *Kids,* and oh my God! That's New York and these are kids who have no supervision. We can be as hyper as we want about pressuring kids, but there are a lot of parents who aren't doing anything at all."

Clark, who survived a scare with breast cancer in 2004 at the age of thirty-seven, made her first post-Einstein project a line of safety videos for kids and families called *The Safe Side,* jointly produced with John Walsh, host of *America's Most Wanted.* As 2007 began, she was focusing on teaching two classes at her daughter's private school. One called "Coffee Shop" covered coffeehouse poetry from the '50s. The other was a literature class that had forced her to refamiliarize herself with *The Lord of the Flies.* She didn't appear to dwell too much on the workings of Baby Einstein, having long ago made peace with the fact that a stable financial future was a trade-off for no longer having any control. But one of the most animated moments of our visit came when she described an idea she had proposed to Disney that had fallen on deaf ears.

"Listen to this," she started in. "You're going to know about this because you're going to have a new baby and you'll have a daughter who's four. And your daughter is going to want to go to Disney World and your wife is going to be pushing the baby all around the hot park wanting to kill herself. So what they should have is a whole Baby Einstein area, which would be really beautiful and really soothing, cool air-conditioned room. They could really market the crap out of it and have Baby Einstein toys all over. They could have big screens playing *Baby Mozart.* It would be *awesome,* wouldn't it?"

Disney executives basically responded, "'We don't care about your idea. We don't want to hear it if it's from you,'" Clark said. "But to me it makes perfect sense. You could have rocking chairs where mothers could nurse their babies. All kinds of people go to Disney theme parks with their preschoolers, and their babies are crying and unhappy and the moms just want to run away screaming."

I gained a sense of the magnitude of Clark's creation of Baby Einstein when I spent time with people in businesses emulating hers. By traveling to Los Angeles and London, I was able to get an up-close view of the emergence of twin twenty-four-hour TV channels aimed at viewers ages three to thirty-six months. Both launched in 2003. Both began in Israel and both are run by husband-and-wife teams with very small children. And, perhaps inevitably, the two became embroiled in lawsuits over copyright issues that as of late 2007 had not been resolved.

The content that both channels air is cheap to produce (most of the animation is done overseas) and easy to package. Segments from two to eight minutes are arranged in endless combinations, everything from wordless, three-dimensional computer animation forays to live-action sign language lessons to animal-themed romps that recall the animated shorts that used to air in American movie theaters. It is not altogether weighty stuff, but, like Baby Einstein, it has a certain built-in appeal to the current generation of parents simply because it has the aura of something customized for their child.

BabyFirstTV is already available in the United States via satellite provider DirecTV, for a premium of $4.99 a month, down from the $9.99 it charged upon launching. BabyTV does not use the subscription model but is aiming to turn a profit on videos and merchandise. It is in forty-five countries, including the United Kingdom and Canada and reportedly planned to go on the air in the United States in the fall of 2007, but no formal announcement had been made as of the summer.

Both channels also have noteworthy owners. News Corporation's Fox International Television recently bought BabyTV, and a big Hollywood production company called New Regency, known for movies such as *Mr. & Mrs. Smith, Fight Club,* and *Heat,* has a one-third stake in BabyFirst. The head of New Regency is an Israeli producer named Arnon Milchan.

When I visited Guy Oranim, the reed-thin head of BabyFirst, whose sand-colored, thinning hair is offset by rectangular-framed glasses, he was dressed in jeans and a blue cotton pullover. He apologized for his outfit, probably because I had worn a suit, but one look at his wrist said it all. He wears a plastic bracelet on his wrist and explains that his wife just had a baby boy, their first child, and his wife was still at the hospital.

BabyFirst launched in the United States on May 11, 2006, on DirecTV, and one month later on Dish Network. It is on a Comcast cable system in Richmond, Virginia, and can be seen in Mexico, Canada, and Puerto Rico. Predictably, there were vociferous objections to its launch, which Oranim shrugged off as merely the utterances of "a lot of opinionated people."

The offices of BabyFirst, in a row of corporate and medical towers along Wilshire Boulevard in West Los Angeles, are low-key. Perhaps there are more primary colors than your average insurance office, but aside from that the company keeps a low profile. Oranim tried to give me a sense of how the channel has evolved. "There are two ways to use the channel: as a babysitter or for parents. People buy this channel for their babies. We got a lot of complaints about parenting content. People told us, 'I don't want to see that stuff when I'm trying to put my baby down to sleep. I want something soothing.' So now we're putting that content into one-to-three-minute clips."

Oranim has a pragmatism and even-tempered approach that is likely the result of the years he spent at giant ad agency BBDO, where his accounts included Similac baby formula. I kept looking at his hospital bracelet, reminding myself that just forty-eight hours earlier he had become a father. As we talked, Oranim's assistant rushed in and presented him with a Post-it Note. He studied it and broke into a smile. "Eight-thirty," he told her in answer to the question on the note—the last time he had fed the baby.

To Oranim, the debate about exposing babies to video or TV content seemed somehow beside the point. His goals as father and businessman should be one.

"This country is so competitive, parents are looking for something to use," he said. "They look backwards to succeed in America. They want their children to have a great job. So to have a great job, they need a great college. To have a great college, they need a great high school. Before high school, it's grade school. And all the way back to when they are a baby. They want to expose him to as many great experiences as they can."

Reading doesn't always get the job done, he explained. "Parents read books to children in a way that's frustrating to them and frustrating to the child. So then they don't read books anymore. There are high-end preschools that give classes on how to read books to kids." With shades of Julie Clark's "video board book" notion, he added, "We want to become the next generation of books."

The role of the channel's education consultant is to "make the channel as boring as possible. Our approach is basic, not rocket science. The medium is not the issue. It's the content. We all can agree that a lettuce salad is healthy for you. But if you eat only lettuce salad, then you will die because it has nothing in it." As to the AAP's recommendation, Oranim said, "We don't disagree with the AAP that parents should interact with their kids. They should." Still, BabyFirst makes no mention of how long babies should be exposed to the channel.

"We thought it would not be wise to state a number," Oranim said. "All kids are different."

Liran Talit, managing director of BabyTV, is far more guarded than Oranim. He and his wife, Maya, work at BabyTV's head-quarters in a gentrifying neighborhood of London called Shep-herd's Bush. Its standard red-brick English row houses are flecked with graffiti and the streets feel just a bit scabby. But it's on the way up. A hip hotel, K West, has been in the area for a while. And Shepherd Studios, a large converted film studio, now houses a range of broadcasters, including Fox Television. Baby TV occu-pies a small glass-walled office situated within the larger Fox operation. The effect, walking into the room, is that of an infant in a hospital nursery, cooing and wriggling behind glass.

As with BabyFirst, it seemed that by effectively going all the way, by staking a claim to being in a baby viewer's consciousness, the executives of BabyTV have in an odd way liberated themselves from caring about the consequences. It isn't that they are callous or blatantly amoral people; they have simply adopted a mind-set that allows them not to be as concerned as most American pre-school producers seem to be.

"Fear is inherent to the discussion of babies and television," reasoned head of programming Ron Isaak. "The way that we live, we detach from nature so much that maybe children are the only thing left for us. People fear television because it's a way of saying good-bye to your child in a way."

A BabyTV "presentation book" shown to investors and the press has one entire page with large letters trumpeting the fact that the channel is "dedicated to babies 24 hours a day" with shows such as *Ping & Pinga,* and *Mr. Snail.* A plasma screen behind Talit's head carried a feed of the channel's endless series of baby enticements, the latest iteration of the anytime playdate.

Talit is the son of an Israeli public relations executive, and his years of learning the family business were often in evidence during our meeting. When I asked him about the baby market and how controversial a channel such as BabyTV was likely to be once it launches in the United States, he shrugged. "We're providing a service," he said. "Parents should make their own decisions about whether to watch with their baby or not."

Knowing that any detail about his hated rivals was likely to get a reaction, I asked whether BabyTV had explored the possibility of something BabyFirst was looking into: having its programs beamed into hospital rooms where babies and new moms recover from birth. He stared at me, speechless, and I realized I had finally found the line Talit would not cross. "Instead of putting the baby to the breast, they're going to put it to BabyFirst?" he said with a smirk. "Good luck to them."

9

CHINESE DEMOCRACY

How Much Mandarin Can a Toddler Take?

A large-screen television sits where fires once roared on the parlor floor of a turn-of-the-century New York brownstone. Real estate agents shopping the multimillion-dollar house would call its marble hearth "original detailing," along with the moldings, parquet floor, and brass sconces. Despite those Gilded Age mementos, the imposing black television and computer in one corner offer clues that it is no longer a period home. In 1975, it was converted into Children's All Day School, one of the elite preschools on Manhattan's Upper East Side.

On the big screen on this bitingly cold day in early March was a stark black-and-white graphic with the phrase "Snowiest Ride." It was the title of an episode of *Ni Hao, Kai-lan,* which was scheduled to begin airing in six months. A handful of the show's twenty-two first-season episodes had passed through the testing process and been sent to Taiwan to be fully animated and colored, but none had yet returned. The deadline pressure was starting to mount. The task for this day at the brownstone was an "animatic" test. A series of still images, edited together with dialogue from the show's actual voice talent, would be screened for a preselected group of preschoolers. This phase of testing follows "storybook" testing, which focuses on the script and the story. Occasionally, fully animated episodes are then tested, but such a luxury is rare and not generally considered useful, since any major problems would be too expensive and time-consuming to fix. In the fast-paced world of series television, especially for a network airing hundreds of new episodes a year, product must remain on the conveyor belt. In the case of *Ni Hao,* once this day's pint-size panel of judges delivered their verdict, there would be no more chances to canvass the audience directly.

Children's All Day is a frequent testing site for Nickelodeon, receiving fees in exchange for providing both space and a selection of kids from the show's target audience. The network rotates shows to a mix of public and private schools, generally in New York and Los Angeles. Some critics have questioned the alliances between the schools and the network. "I remember coming here for *Blue's Clues,*" recalls *Ni Hao* head writer Sascha Paladino, who also wrote episodes for *Blue's.* With a nod to a wall rack, he added, "It looks like they get a lot of free tapes."

Arrayed on the room's wood floor, in a neatly spaced semi-circle, were ten fully disassembled Mr. Potato Head toys for the kids to play with as the episode unfolded. In the room were five adults: Paladino, educational consultant Christine Ricci, Nickelodeon production executive Elly Kramer, show publicist Sharyn Traub, and myself. Paladino sat on a couch at the back of the room. Traub and I sat in chairs in another corner in the back and Ricci and Kramer flanked the television, facing the children so they could "score" the session, noting where attention lagged or questions arose. A camcorder on a tripod stood unobtrusively in another corner.

The mood was tenser than the focus group in Glendale, which came at a very preliminary stage, "when we didn't even know what the show was," Paladino said. "The goal today is to see how much Chinese we can put into the episodes without losing" the kids, said Ricci, a tall, forthright brunette. The test had not been scheduled until recently, but Nickelodeon wanted to make sure it was on course with the Chinese component. The curriculum was also an unusual one for preschool TV. Rather than teaching academic principles, problem-solving, or "learning through play," *Ni Hao* was zeroing in on toddlers' emotions. Episodes revolved around maintaining self-confidence, conquering fear, helping others—important components of a child's development, certainly, but seldom the sole focus of an entire series. Big Bird may have had his arc during *Sesame Street* when he would address such matters, but a typical episode would also tackle counting, tying shoes, and hopscotch. Despite their abiding conviction that the curriculum was timely and essential, those behind *Ni Hao* were anxious about whether their audience would embrace it. When kids strongly embrace a show's signature—Blue's pawprint clues, Dora's multicolored adventures, the Little Einsteins' rocket ship exploration—their bond propels the show to hit status. Without their emotional identification, shows languish. Unlike the movies or prime-time television, where flops vanish quickly, in the preschool world most shows get at least a few months to prove themselves. The dial is therefore full of zombie shows lurching onward, episode after episode, without ever fulfilling their highest educational potential or spawning profitable toy lines or theme-park rides.

Producers were also struggling with the pesky little issue of deadlines. With the show in limbo for a time, the network had seen the show make strides since January 2007 and had put it back on the official schedule for a late August debut. Barely five months from the day of the Children's All Day focus group, the series was supposed to be up and running. Ambitious and maybe even reckless, but that was the plan.

The door opened, and in walked six three-year-olds, ushered by Kramer. Ricci motioned for them to sit down in front of the TV.

"Hi, I'm Christine and I work at Nickelodeon," she told them. "I brought a video for you today. It's a brand-new show, so new that it isn't even on TV yet. Do you want to watch it?" They nodded. "Now we're still working on it, so it isn't colored in yet. When it goes on TV, it'll be all colored in. When you're watching, you can play, talk, stand up, whatever you want. Just no touching anyone, and no hitting. OK? OK." She started the DVD player.

The screen filled with black-and-white images and the story began. As in every episode, Kai-lan exhorts the viewer to help her wake up the sun. Then she looks at outside and sees that it has snowed. She and Grampa start playing with the snow, shoveling it into the air and identifying it repeatedly with the Mandarin word *xue* (pronounced "schwiye"). She turned to address the camera. "Do you want to know how I say 'snow' in Chinese? Xue. Say it!" (She waits, motionless, employing the interactivity pause pioneered by *Blue's Clues*.) "You sound just like me!" A boy named Nicholas, dressed in a black polo shirt and khakis, smiled at the word. He kept repeating it to himself, like the punch line to his own private joke. "That's funny!" he concluded.

In essence, the episode's plot concerns Tolee, a koala, being afraid to sled down a steep hill. He learns that by working his way up to it "little by little by little," with the support of his friends, he can overcome his fear and have fun in the snow. It reminded me of a book called *Stella, Queen of the Snow,* an old favorite of Margot's. The series of *Stella* books feature a redheaded girl and her little brother, Sam, who is a resolutely circumspect boy. He asks a million questions and is tentative about trying anything.

Most of the children were absorbed by the action on-screen. Nicholas was in and out. In the show's final third, he announced, "I am going to play with toys," and did just that for the remaining time.

When the episode ended, Ricci addressed the group again. "OK, so what happened in that video?" One child ventured, "Tolee got scared." Ricci read a few more questions from a single prepared page. "Do you remember how she said 'thank you' in Chinese?" The question hung there for a few pregnant seconds until a girl said, "Xia, xia." Ricci followed quickly, "And how do you say 'snow' in Chinese?" The word had taken up about thirty seconds in an exchange between Kai-lan and Grampa, each of whom said it twice. Still, none of the children answered. Ricci's training dictated she betray no emotion. "That's OK!" she said, trying to sound chipper. Kramer scribbled intently. "Can you tell me what was your favorite part?" That question drew plenty of responses—"when they got over the bumps," "when she got on the sled," "riding on the sled." That brought the questions to a close and the group was excused.

Paladino seemed a little troubled by the fact that the Chinese did not register. "We shouldn't have done *xe* and *xue xue* in the same episode," he said. "There are so many things about this episode that make me think, 'Ohh . . .'" Ricci and Kramer studied their notes. "I was looking at that one boy," Traub said, meaning Nicholas, the detached one. "And I was thinking, 'Well, that's the future.'" Would that be the future for *Ni Hao, Kai-lan*? To be a well-made diversion, playing in the background as toddlers play with their toys?

The next of the day's three groups would not exactly ease that worry. Ages four and five, they came in and sat in a straight line facing the TV, the last time they would be anything close to orderly. When Ricci told them she was about to show them a video, a tall boy named Louis cut her off in mid-sentence. "I have this movie at my dad's house," he said proudly. "This movie is so new it isn't even on TV yet," Ricci said. "But I have it!" Louis insisted. Ricci forged ahead, delivered the rest of her spiel, and started the disc.

As his classmates watched the screen, Louis immediately started fiddling with the Potato Head pieces. When the character called HoHo was introduced, he muttered, "What's HoHo?" The others repeated the word *xue* right on cue, and when Kai-lan has to fill in a bare patch of dirt with snow so she can use her sled, they pointed right at the dirt patch.

At the ten-minute mark, Louis began leading an insurrection. He first distracted his neighbor by showing him his Mr. Potato Head. They began to play, and then two playing became three, four, and eventually all five children in the room. When the video started, they were sitting in a straight line about five feet from the screen. Fifteen minutes later, they were ten feet away and at one point all of them had their backs to the screen. They swapped plastic potatoes, showed off their hybrid variations, and generally displayed no interest in the show. One boy, the red lights on his shoes blinking frequently, hopped between one end of the row and the other. Spying magic markers and paper, he asked the group, "Do you want to draw?" No one replied, but he began scribbling anyway.

Paladino, who usually wears an imperturbable expression,

looked slightly vexed. Ricci and Kramer exchanged an annoyed look. The video, mercifully, came to an end. It took almost five minutes to separate the kids from their toys and get them to return to their original position. Once they were there, the question-and-answer period proved nearly useless. "How did Kai-lan say 'thank you' in Chinese?" Ricci asked. She waited, but no answer came. "Do you remember how you said 'snow' in Chinese?" Ricci asked. Again, no answer. "What was your favorite part of the video?" After another silent moment, a child responded: "I want to go back." And so they did. Kramer led them out of the room and the adults who remained let out a sigh.

"Tough crowd," Paladino said, speaking for the room. "In terms of the Chinese, Christine, are we going to look at pages and see what lost them or what was working?" Paladino asked. "It's hard to tell from that group." In previous months, Nickelodeon Preschool president Brown Johnson had expressed some concern about preschoolers being able to absorb the language aspect of the show. "Pronunciation is so specific in Mandarin. There are all of these 'aouhhhh,' 'ohhh' tones," she said, imitating the language's tones, dissonant to the Western ear, which connote specific meanings of words. "So when the girl who plays Kai-lan records, she sounds like she's yelling at Grampa because Mandarin is kind of a brittle, aggressive language. So we'd say, 'Can she say that with a little more smile in her voice?' 'No.' It just is what it is."

They all chuckled ruefully, recalling how convinced Louis was that he already had seen the episode and how intent he was on causing a disruption. "You sometimes get kids who talk in a way that seems way older than their age," Paladino said. "We were out in L.A., where obviously a lot of preschoolers have parents in the entertainment business, and this one kid told us that the show had story problems. He was breaking it down like Robert McKee in a screenwriting class. 'You know, you need a villain to give it a little more conflict.'"

The next and final group filed in—seven kids ages three and four. They immediately appeared more orderly than the last group. From Ricci's introduction right through the opening scenes of the episode, they sat attentively and focused on the fireplace. As fate would have it, though, the most patient group of subjects had to endure a near-biblical spate of distractions and interruptions. A teacher opened the door at one point and pointedly asked Kramer if the group had reserved the room and how long they planned to stay. Kramer patiently explained what was happening and the woman left. Then a garbage truck picking its way along East sixteenth Street whirred and clattered, and cars stuck behind it let out elongated honks. A folk singer slinging an acoustic guitar passed through the room on the way to the school's baby nursery, pausing to slip blue sterile booties over his shoes. The muffled sounds of his strumming and singing could soon be heard from the next room. The goal of maintaining a neutral space where the pure reactions of test subjects could be assessed suddenly seemed out the window.

The unspoken question: How would the test subjects react to all this chaos? Would it be reflected in their reactions?

Ricci went through her paces, gauging reactions. "Do you remember how to say 'snow' in Chinese?" she asked. No one answered, but one boy pointed to an Asian classmate named Tyler, implying he would know the answer.

"What was your favorite part of the video?" Ricci asked. The kids all jumped in. "Big mountain sledding!" said one. "Ice sculptures!" said another. Then a boy named Jonathan said his favorite part was "the shark." One of the others rejoined, "Hey, there's no shark in the movie!" Ricci reminded everyone, "It's OK, everyone can remember it how they want." The line sounded like an unofficial mantra of focus groups.

As the children filed out, I kept comparing what I had witnessed, probably unfairly, to legendary stories about preschool research landmarks—*Sesame Street, Blue's Clues, Dora*. People had shared stories that resembled religious experiences—roomfuls of the converted, shouting and testifying. I had seen video footage of *Blue's Clues* tests where kids stood, hopped up and down, pointed and cheered, their eyes never leaving the screen. This was research nirvana, the moment when the manufacturer recognizes that their product is unequivocally going to connect with its intended audience.

The *Ni Hao* tests didn't approach that exalted level, but the group remained resolute. Ricci was determined to remain upbeat. "They held in pretty well considering all the distractions," she said. No one disagreed with her out loud, but there was still no empirical sense that the show in which they had invested so much of themselves would hit the mark.

Four hours later, the picture got a bit clearer at Nickelodeon's Times Square headquarters. The *Ni Hao* group had reconvened there for a "debrief" in a corner conference room on the thirty-eighth floor. Floor-to-ceiling windows afforded spectacular views of the Hudson River to the west, the Empire State Building to the south, and the Chrysler Building to the east. Ricci distributed a bar chart showing the focus groups' attention during each minute of the episode to Paladino, Kramer, and production exec Kay Wilson Stallings. A large, bound stack of legal-sized sheets contained each of the twenty-four frames of the twenty-three-minute episode, heavily annotated with the three focus groups' reactions. On the speakerphone from Burbank, California, were the other key members of the show's team, among them producer Mary Harrington, creator-producer Karen Chau, and writer Bradley Zweig.

Researchers generally define "attention" as any time when children's eyes are on-screen, a quality they learn to judge with experience. The attention graph for "Snowiest Ride" resembled stairs down, with steady levels through the first ten minutes, then a dip toward the middle, back up again, and then a downtrend through the final minutes. One positive sign: on a scale of 0 to 20, the bars in the first one-third of the episode consistently hit 15, 16, or even 18.

Still, a range of worries came to the surface, and they all attested to the unusually difficult balancing act of *Ni Hao, Kai-lan*. The show was trying to be equal parts cultural and language exchange, behavioral model, and vividly illustrated laugh riot. "There were a few places that I didn't think *Kai-lan* was TV-safe," Ricci said, referring to the problem of characters slipping out of the visual frame and therefore compromising the educational content. "Also, we kept hearing the kids say 'little by little' but it was hard to pull any other words out of them. We need to be careful that the music doesn't all sound the same because we are leading the audience through a thought process. They need to understand what 'little by little' means." A conversation followed about the little ditties—dubbed "takeaways"—that will be sprinkled into each episode. A composer was still working on those short musical passages, aping the tactics of shows from the dawn of television that used music to reinforce characters and lessons. When the voice tracks were recorded for the animatic tests, the actors said their lines straight and did not sing any passages.

"The interactive material doesn't feel as central to the story, so they don't care about it as much," said Harrington. "This is such a different show, though," Ricci responded. "When we've tested this with parents, they've told us that they really want a social curriculum. Education is fine, but what they really want is social skills." Harrington asked about games within the show that could be made more interactive. "Kids get tired of 'do you see?' so we have to think about some other games," she said. "That's what we found with the game where kids match Chinese symbols. It's a creative game and matching is fun, but it's also full of Chinese cultural content." Harrington, pressed on, displaying her commercial instincts from *Rugrats* and other animated landmarks for older kids. She knew that success demanded honest appraisal of even the things assumed to be most sacred. The beginning moments of each episode, in which Kai-lan gets the audience to help her wake up the sun, had been in place for at least a year and a half. Nevertheless, Harrington asked, "Does the moment with the sun take too long and get boring?" In New York, there was a pause as people looked at one another, momentarily taken aback. "Every show has a different way of doing things," Ricci said. "*Dora, Diego,* and *Little Einsteins* have an opening question that they pursue for the rest of the episode. We're doing it more with movement." Paladino added, "We know kids love that, from all the tests we've done. Attention levels at the morning focus group hit seventeen or eighteen during the sun moments." "Leave it in," Ricci said. "It's not hurting the scores. Going forward, we should try to make something else feel a little more interactive if this doesn't feel like it's delivering that."

The sun moment was one of the program's "formal features"—events or exchanges of dialogue or song that occur at the same interval in every show. The formal features are like tent poles that hold up the changeable fabric of the episodes. Harrington, continuing to balance the comparative restraints of preschool television with her desire to make a show that's fun, asked about one of the formal features, the exchange at the end of each episode between Kai-lan and Grampa. "I think it's sometimes a little unfortunate that there is that moment at the end, after we've been having so much fun. That intimate, talking moment sometimes feels a little boring. We've just come from something much more exciting and then we're back with YeYe, while the kids are off having so much more fun."

There was some general agreement, especially given the steep decline in the attention bars during the moment with YeYe. But some in New York noted how culturally appropriate the formal feature was, under the guidance of the show's Chinese cultural consultant and, of course, Karen Chau. The intergenerational relationship would be a rare one in the realm of preschool TV, but also an important message to send to developing kids. Harrington's note was definitely taken, but for now the "YeYe moment" would stay, only hopefully with more entertainment value. Ricci later noted how the team behind *Dora the Explorer* labored to develop the show-ending formal feature, which has Dora asking the viewer, "What was your favorite part of the adventure?"—a conscious echo of the focus-group protocol. When Paladino asked her whether it was normal to have a dropoff in attention at the very end of a show, Ricci said, "Why do you think we added those credit games on *Dora?*" She was referring to the split screen showing, on one side, the credits and, on the other, a game with the cursor where the viewer has to spot Tico, Swiper, or another character who hides and then peeks out again in different spots on the screen.

The discussion moved to a more positive topic: favorable ratings for the show's eclectic supporting cast. The consensus was that the show was offering a full banquet for audiences, not just one lead character. For where would Dora be without Boots?

Someone even suggested allowing some of the minor characters to have interactive moments with the audience.

Ricci, normally the one trying to rally enthusiasm, found herself playing a little defense. "I get nervous when you're using them for entertainment value," she said. "We don't want to throw them in just to make her look interesting. It's her show. She should be interesting in and of herself."

As the call wound to a close, Wilson Stallings made a provocative suggestion. "One thing we can do next year is do a big postmort," she said. "We can take four or five episodes and do a minute-by-minute ratings analysis. Some of these ideas we can strategically start to implement in the second season." Paladino asked, "With actual ratings?" She replied, "Oh yeah, we can just go through everything to see when it dips and comes back up and what people are responding to."

There was a beat as everyone digested the notion of being on for another season, having more time to think about changes, even the idea of having actual ratings, in other words, actually being on the air. "That's a great idea!" a voice from Burbank blurted out.

In reality, a definitive call on green-lighting another season would not be made until the ratings were in on the first season. "It's in the interest of speed that I even mentioned it," Wilson Stallings said later. "Things happen really fast, so if there is a pickup you have to be prepared."

As the session started to disband, I approached Ricci and asked her how the scores for *Ni Hao* compared with the other shows she had worked on. She shrugged. "We've figured out a pretty good formula," Ricci said, "at least for today's generation. I don't know how we'll figure out the next one."

Two days later, on March 8, Brown Johnson and her troops at Nickelodeon Preschool gathered at the Nokia Theatre to make their pitch to advertisers. It was the annual "up-front" sales presentation, the biggest chance for the network to make its case as the destination for any advertiser interested in reaching kids. While Noggin is not ad-supported, Nick Jr. shows like *Ni Hao, Kai-lan,* as well as *Dora, Backyardigans,* and *Wonder Pets!,* would be broadcast on "Big Nick" during the daily preschool block, which is ad-supported. Even in the ad-free environment of Noggin, a lot depends on the strength of ad sales at the parent company and their shows get plugged along with fare for older kids. In a reorganization in 2006 that involved hundreds of layoffs companywide, Johnson assumed a new title and properties were realigned such that preschool and older-kid fare mixed together more than they had before in terms of marketing and promotion.

Johnson took a turn, introducing new shows *Yo Gabba Gabba!,* a hip-hop-fueled *Banana Splits*-esque show with a retro magazine format, and *Ni Hao.* A short clip reel played, a hyperkinetic jumble designed to match the breakneck pace of the morning. Johnson mentioned a new Web community with shades of virtual world Second Life called Nicktropolis, which had attracted a million registrations. Her series descriptions were kept brief, to allow more time for older-kid shows. After Johnson spoke, the event moved rapidly through its paces—a cameo by George Lopez, whose sitcom had been picked up by Nickelodeon's Nick at Nite block; a plug for *iCarly,* a new tween show that would incorporate user-generated content; and, finally, a ragged performance by the Naked Brothers Band, stars of a new series by that name. The wall that Geraldine Layboume had described between big-kid fare and preschool seemed more porous than ever.

10

LIVE ACTS

"If You're Old Enough to Walk, You're Old Enough to Rock"

The frescoes on the walls in the room where the Hayes family stayed in Florence, Italy, stretched fifteen feet up to the ceiling, depicting all manner of Renaissance scenes—fruit tree forests, tempting snakes, wise men reading from scrolls. It was *Where the Wild Things Are* with biblical references. Traveling in the off-season, we had found a decent rate in a spectacular 16th century villa about two hundred yards from Piazza della Signoria, down one of the city's many cobblestone streets. Through the villa's oversize door with a round, half-ring handle in the middle, and stone entryway, a courtyard beckoned with a fountain and ivy-covered walls. It looked more or less as it did in Michelangelo's day.

Breaking the old-world spell, Margot made repeated use of the room's CD player, spinning a favorite title from home called *Dance Fiesta!*, a spin-off from *Dora the Explorer.* The voices of

Dora, Boots, Swiper, & Co. belted out G-rated covers of "The Rhythm Is Gonna Getcha," "Celebration," and "Locomotion." The music did not float easily into adult ears. Dora could peel paint off the walls with cries such as "Now, it's your turn, Back-pack!!!" (Just as on television, there were exclamation points on every line.) Margot was enraptured. Although she was barely two years old, her addiction to this CD was profound. She would dance to it late at night, wake up to it, eat to it, bathe to it. The 223rd rendition of the Go-Go's "We Got the Beat" was performed with even more zest than the first.

I nevertheless felt great relief that Margot, for practically the first time since infancy, had a new entertainment obsession that did not involve a screen. No psychological studies have, as yet, been conducted about the effects of music on very young listeners. For me, music has always served as a source of stimulation by stirring my imagination without filling in too many blanks. A lyric or melody could suggest many things, but it always allowed some interpretation, some active mental participation, in a way that a TV episode generally does not. As a committed audiophile and son of a onetime radio DJ, I found Margot getting into music to be not only sensible but worthy of encouragement. As I would come to discover, an entire industry has blossomed around that very sentiment.

Once the blighted province of a few dusty copies of Raffi and *Barney* soundtracks, the kids-music shelf now groans under new weight. Artists such as Dan Zanes or Laurie Berkner are making gold and near-platinum albums and selling out Carnegie Hall. Established draws from They Might Be Giants to Lisa Loeb to avant-jazz outfit Medeski Martin and Wood also have recorded kids albums. Compilations feature tracks from the likes of Low, Flaming Lips, Tom Waits, Cake, Nada Surf, and Wilco. Tie-in CDs for shows like *Wonder Pets!* or *Little Einsteins* (a Disney series that often uses sophisticated classical tracks in plots of episodes) are de rigeur, and kids sections of big-box stores are expanding accordingly. An East Coast tour of a group of preschool artists called Jamarama Live!, initially a joint venture with Noggin, was packaged by Hollywood's omnipotent Creative Artists Agency, better known for representing Steven Spielberg and Brad Pitt. "We've gotten great response from companies and parents," said Jenna Adler of CAA, a mother of two toddlers who conceived of the tour, which lets companies sell CDs and DVDs in the lobby. "But one interesting thing we found was that open-floor seating was a big turnoff. Music fans who stood through a concert at Roseland Ballroom when they were in college definitely want a comfy seat when they're with their kids."

The Web site of Jamarama Live! conveys a slogan whose syntax is murky but whose message is clear: "If you're old enough to walk, you're old enough to ROCK! And even if you can't walk just yet, you can still ROCK!" That conviction is at the heart of the spiraling popularity of preschool music, which is occurring in a larger industry experiencing a legendary slump. For one, music promotion is infinitely more targeted than in past decades. There is, for example, an XM Satellite Radio channel dedicated to preschool music. Blogs and digital downloads allow music to be shared and passed along, something parents do with abandon when it comes to other aspects of parenting. Also, music videos have made convenient filler for commercial-free networks such as the Disney Channel or Sprout or Noggin.

After I confided in friends and fellow parents about hearing Dora sing "La Bamba" 412 times one rainy weekend, one of them had a suggestion: Milkshake. People who know preschool TV know Milkshake because their videos can be seen on PBS Kids

Sprout, Discovery Kids, and Noggin. Milkshake was founded in 2003 by two longtime musicians in an alt-pop Baltimore band called Love Riot, Lisa Mathews and Mikel Gehl. Their sound is an appealing stew of 10,000 Maniacs, the B-52's, and Camper Van Beethoven, with lyrics and songs completely dedicated to kids topics like playing baseball, counting to ten, learning the alphabet, and pretending to be in the ocean or outer space. The band manages the feat of sounding sophisticated enough to lure adults but kid-friendly enough to interest kids. That this duality is even possible today owes something to the fact that many top preschool music acts had first careers as grown-up pop artists—Zanes used to front college-rock outfit the Del Fuegos; "Farmer Jason" is the kiddie alias of Jason Ringenberg of country–hard rock band Jason and the Scorchers, of songs such as "Broken Whiskey Glass" and "Hot Nights in Georgia."

Margot immediately clicked with Milkshake. Her favorite track was called "School." It was an up-tempo, vaguely New Wavey track with a skittering drum loop and squalling guitars, whose chorus she quickly learned to sing along to: "I can't wait to get back to school / No matter what other kids say, I have a lot of fun / When we're learning things here at school / I bet anyone can see we have a lot of fun." She and I have seen Milkshake perform three times now, and they put on a high-energy show. The uncanny thing, for me as a music fan and veteran of many club shows, is how similar the overall vibe is, though the lights are always kept on and the refreshment stand stocks only juices and cookies. But the band keeps things moving with costume changes, props, and sing-alongs. A frenzied, mirthful mini mosh pit of toddlers always rims the stage, sometimes piling up onto it. Parents play bouncer, helping kids down from the stage when the action gets too intense.

After one show that I caught without Margot, I stuck around as the band loaded up its gear into the small SUV it had driven up from Baltimore. Someone's iPod was now plugged into the sound system, so now Metallica's "Master of Puppets" boomed out of the speakers instead of "Bottle of Sunshine" and "Happy Song." Minus the teeming hordes of toddlers, it felt like the stage could have been anywhere and the band another seasoned touring act. The manager of the venue came up to report ticket sales—brisk, about three-quarters capacity. Not unaccustomed to selling out, Gehl asked the manager what he thought prevented a sellout. "Well, Justin Roberts [a fellow preschool rocker] had a show today, so that was tough. But I'm happy, I think people were really into it." Gehl and Mathews nodded in agreement. The band finished loading up and then let me tag along as it headed off to a nearby restaurant to eat, drink, and unwind. It could have been called an after-party but somehow that didn't seem right given the time: half past noon.

Mathews, the lithe, auburn-haired lead vocalist whose onstage trademark is a multicolored tutu, scrunched up her face when I mentioned Margot's favorite Milkshake song, "School." "Do you know there's a mistake in that song?" she asked, looking uncomfortable. I told her that yes, because we had heard it probably more than one hundred times in the past couple of months, especially in the car where close listening is possible, I had noticed. When she and Mikel engage in school-themed, spoken-word banter toward the end of the track, she says, "Mikel, what do you get when you add up all the numbers on a clock?" He responds, "Seventy-two!" And she says, "Yeah, and it's my grandfather's age!" The real answer, as eggheads everywhere know, is seventy-eight. Discovering this damaged my opinion of Milkshake not one iota. But for Mathews, it was mortifying. "We can't go back and fix it now, so I just have to keep explaining it to everyone!" she said.

Mathews and Gehl, who both had children with their respective partners in 2001, told me they decided to form Milkshake in 2003. "When we started Milkshake, I thought we would do a new CD every two years, giving us time to reflect on our children's growth and draw direct inspiration from them," Mathews said. "I wasn't sure this would work, since this meant that each CD would have to leave childhood behind eventually. So far, I think we are reflecting our children's growth, but our new CD, *Play*, seems to speak to three- and four-year-olds alongside our five- and six-year olds. It remains to be seen if the next CD will still do so. Because it will be based on fairy tales, it might because a good story spans the ages. Mikel and I used to have a ten-year plan. We would put out five CDs and our children would be ten and that would be it. Now we feel like we will make music for children as long as we have something viable to say. There is so very much more to write about when you are in a child's realm versus an adult's. And we are having so much fun playing for and with the kids."

After ten years in Love Riot, the pair felt ready for a change, though playing gigs in some respects was easier then. "You could just play and go, 'Uhhh,'" Mathews said, miming a zoned-out guitar hero. "But with kids you have to have your energy up all the time."

Gehl, who wears a button-down shirt with a rainbow-colored, pinwheel-like pattern for each gig, doesn't speak like a missionary, but ask him about his calling and it readily reveals itself. "I feel like it's us doing this music versus the rest of the music business. There were plenty of people who told me I was out of my mind when we started this. They said, 'Do you know how much children's CDs represent in total CD sales? One-half of one percent!' And I'm like, 'Well . . . ' But it was time for a change. It seemed like a generational change, just like there was when punk rock happened. It was time. Those kids were becoming parents and it was time for their kids' music to reflect a change."

Milkshake and other bands, while dependent on TV outlets for exposure, are aiming for a different kind of entertainment experience, something that involves no focus groups and requires no young fan to sit still for twenty-two minutes. That was what I responded to—the idea of interrupting Margot's well-entrenched cycle of entertainment stimulation. "When we were on tour with Dan Zanes, it was cool because we'd talk philosophically about what we're doing," said Gehl, a meditative guitarist with shoulder-length brown hair who cites Michael Hedges as a major influence. "It's funny because you never get a chance to talk like that with another artist unless you're stuck in an airport for three hours. Even though our music's different, we both had this idea that Madison Avenue sees society as a series of customers. There's this demographic and this demographic. They try to divide us that way. What Dan Zanes is doing and what we're doing is we want to bring families together and parents can come with their kids and the kids saying, 'I love this!' and the parents saying, 'I love this too!' And everyone's having a good time."

In just the four years since the band was formed, Mathews has noticed a significant evolution of the preschool entertainment landscape. "Noggin didn't so much worry about what kids were going to learn," she said. "But now they have these little announcements about what the kids are going to learn in each show. But it's the kids watching, not really the parents."

When Milkshake got a plum assignment from PBS to write some interstitial music, "They were worried about our looks," said Mathews, whose hair is often streaked with different colors, in a subtle nod to her postpunk roots. "They didn't want my combat boots or the tights. They said, 'How about Converse high-tops?' I'm like, 'That's as far as I'll go.' My friend who brought the *Teletubbies* to BBC told me for the British crowd I was perfect but Mikel would need to cut his hair."

Mathews thought for a moment. "They're trying to fit into a certain decorum. They say, 'With this hair, does this look acceptable?' And they run all these tests. Milkshake doesn't run any tests. We just go out there. Are the kids happy? Do they like what we're doing and are we reaching them? We can tell when they come up to the stage like they did today and they want to be part of it. Kids need to shut down sometimes."

One of the key ingredients, Mathews and Gehl agreed, was engaging a child's imagination without painting the whole picture for them. "For example, I like the Wiggles and I take my son to see the Wiggles, but sometimes it feels too completist, like it fills in too many blanks," Gehl said. "Let the child fill in some of those blanks."

It was interesting to compare notes about television and kids with Gehl and Mathews, as both entertainers and fellow parents.

"My son watched one or two hours a day" when he was a toddler, Gehl said. "I was never one of those musicians who had a bumper sticker that said, 'Throw out your TV.' I think TV's great. It just depends on how much you watch and what you watch."

He added, "I don't get this baby TV. That's horrible. I'm sorry, but babies should not watch TV. Just do your job as a mom or dad and take care of that kid."

Mathews said fans often ask if Milkshake will put out a DVD. "We will, but I want ours to be something different," she said. "I want it to maybe be in black and white because kids don't usually get to see anything in black and white. Kids will be able to watch it over and over, of course, but at least it will look a little different."

The element that Milkshake and other preschool music acts can offer, of course, is the live experience. Gehl recalled a Fourth of July show in 2005 in the suburbs of Washington, D.C. "We were headlining, performing as a duo," he said. "There was a huge crowd, several thousand people. And kids were really getting into it, so we said, 'OK, we're going to ask a few kids to come onstage.' Well, it was a bum rush. Two or three hundred kids jammed onto the stage [Lisa interjects: "That's when I said, 'We need liability insurance and we need it now!'"] and next came the fire marshal. We were embarrassed. The fire marshal came by and we said, 'OK, you guys are going to have to go back to your seats.' That's rock and roll. That's what we said. We said any duo, a guy with a guitar and a woman singer and a tambourine that can get hundreds of kids riled up like that is worth remembering. It was cool. It was one of those out-of-control moments that you couldn't make up."

I couldn't help but recall the relative purity of the Milkshake shows when I took Margot to a pair of musical stage shows at Radio City Music Hall that were their complete antithesis and existed to expand revenues for television shows. The first, *Barney Live,* crammed about twenty songs into ninety minutes. Somehow, it was almost as if the famously vast Radio City stage forced the show to move extra fast. The show's story was about a place called the T-Rific Toy Factory, which comes equipped with an Imagination Machine capable of fixing the broken ballerina and airplane toys that were revealed in the opening scene. A song emphasizing the urgency of cranking up the machine had a blunt lyric that became stuck in my head for days: "There's nothing worse than a broken toy." Merchandise is the goal and the show seems to have succeeded on that score—the lobby teemed with families hauling off coloring books, plush dolls, and all manner of Barney-iana.

Along with the short dinosaur accomplices, there were two human players who lip-synched every line of dialogue and the words to every song. They were young-looking, maybe in their early twenties, and dressed casually. The gimmick was that they both worked at the T-Rific Toy Factory and throughout the show they brought out toys and sets and playthings—a farm, musical instruments, a rocket ship bearing dancing robots. The bits and songs were short and direct and the whole show boomed out of speaker towers with a canned, syncopated beat and instrumentation. Many of the families sang and clapped along; they knew the words by heart. The lights occasionally cast patterns on the ceiling—hearts, stars, candy. At one point a rain barrel in the farm was full of candy, not rain, and the walls became papered with candy silhouettes. After the "I Love You, You Love Me" finale, there was a popping sound (not too loud) and heart-shaped confetti rained down on the crowd.

At a preshow photo op for media guests, Margot reacted badly to the idea of getting her picture taken with Barney ("I want to go home!" she screamed, and the photo with Barney shows her discomfort) but she ended up warming to the show, bopping along to the music, eating Goldfish and asking, when it was all over, "Where's Barney?" The real imprint seemed to be that plush Barney doll from a goodie bag we had gotten at the preshow reception. She clutched the doll tightly in her hand on the walk to the subway, then during our entire stay at the playground, and right on until bedtime.

Our next visit to Radio City was for *Diego Live*, a sub–*Lion King* extravaganza with Latin rhythms and tropical, two-dimensional set designs, which left Margot a little perplexed despite her ardor for *Go, Diego, Go!* on television. The interactive elements of the show were pumped up even more onstage, with barely a minute passing without Diego exhorting the crowd to answer simple pop quizzes or "say it louder!" As with most brand extensions, the show's creators in most cases do not directly oversee stage shows, but they can look in on them as they develop.

Margot didn't respond in full voice until the latter part of the show, and when the audience was called upon to do physical actions, such as miming a jaguar scratching a tree, Margot stood still and studied the stage. The plot concerned Baby Jaguar losing her growl to a pair of "bobos," the show's unexplained synonym for monkeys. Diego and Baby Jaguar (aided by Dora) traveled to an ancient pyramid, found the bobos, and got the jaguar's growl back. As with Barney, the show squeezed in about two dozen songs (all the better to move soundtracks during intermission) such as "Special, Especial (Everyone Is Special)." The formula was undoubtedly a successful one, as revenue totaled $4.3 million for the run at Radio City, breaking the record for a family-audience touring show that had been set in 2003 by Diego's cousin, Dora the Explorer.

Long after the show, I kept thinking of the bobos, which seemed an odd choice as the name of a couple of primate characters. I looked it up, but could find no other usage of the word except for a recent coinage as a mildly derisive term short for "bourgeois bohemians" popularized by David Brooks in his book *Bobos in Paradise*. The book had already illuminated the contemporary American society built from the combination of '60s rebellion and '80s materialism. Come to think of it, this was the same generation that had the hunger and means to create accelerated, test-marketed, multifaceted edutainment for babies and toddlers. Maybe it was a pretty good name for these characters after all.

11

DELAYED EDIFICATION

Kai-lan Finally Enters the Living Room

After four long and winding years in development and production, Kai-lan at last met her public at an idiosyncratic television industry ritual known as "press tour," which the Television Critics Association (TCA) stages twice a year in Los Angeles. Dozens of TV networks—from the big broadcasters on down to the most marginal of cable outposts—give presentations of their upcoming rosters, highlighting their major shows. They also offer journalists from a range of print and online outlets a chance to interview creators, executives, and stars. They throw lavish parties. The TCA hands out awards for the best shows already on the air. The whole process takes about a week and a half.

Sometimes, actual news breaks, if only because sequestered journalists are eager to create some. When CBS used a press tour to present the reality show *Kid Nation,* about a group of minors who run their own town in New Mexico, it became a major story. Aside from such glimmers of excitement, press tour is an experience not unlike walking past an endless row of car dealerships, and getting trapped briefly at each one for a hurried pitch before you are hustled to the next.

In July 2007, press tour was held at the Beverly Hilton. The mid-'60s hotel is known for Merv Griffin's lengthy ownership and a poolside environment that agreeably evokes the heyday of Bob Hope and the Rat Pack. The Beverly Hilton's International Ballroom, where the movie world's A-list gathers each year for the Golden Globe Awards, drinking, schmoozing, and celebrating at intimate round tables, was transformed for press tour into an office-like bullpen. Straight rows of mostly male, mostly bespectacled, mostly white writers replaced the round banquet tables of Hollywood royalty. Most of the hundred or so writers kept their laptops open and spent most of the sessions tapping out notes and stories, bathed in a blue glow. Clips of shows, or slickly edited "sizzle reels" designed to promote them, filled giant screens on either side of the stage. Brief panel discussions with the producers, creators, and actors from each show, loosely moderated by each network's executives, accompanied the footage. The panels consisted almost entirely of questions from the audience, a forum that has been used for many years at TCA but can leave the networks vulnerable to bizarre, tangential, or acerbic questions from cooped-up writers. One example from TV Land's session: "If Elvis were alive today, would he be downloading music? Would he have an iPod?"

MTV Networks, Viacom's large subsidiary whose twelve cable channels include Nickelodeon, TV Land, MTV, VH1, Spike, and CMT (Country Music Television), held the stage from 9 A.M. to noon. Like press tour in general, the featured shows spanned a wide range, from a sniper drama starring John Leguizamo called *Kill Point* to self-explanatory reality show *Ty Murray's Celebrity*

Bull-Riding Challenge. Each network came out, did its spiel, and then handed the baton to the next. TCA staff rearranged furniture and microphones with the alacrity and precision of Broadway stagehands. The spotlight would go down for a few seconds and come back up on the next attraction. The overall effect was one of live-action channel surfing.

Into this disorienting setting, absent any of the trappings of research or kid-centric culture that defined its creation, stepped *Ni Hao, Kai-lan*. Brown Johnson, using a script written by head writer Sascha Paladino, gave a brief introduction to a three-minute sizzle reel. "We're here to present our next learning journey," Johnson said. "This fall, millions of preschoolers will learn Mandarin Chinese." The lights dimmed and the reel lit up large screens on either side of the stage. *"Ni Hao, Kai-lan* will help preschoolers identify the emotions they're feeling," a narrator said. The video showed a scene from "Dragonboat Festival," an early episode. "When you feel mad, the first thing you do is calm, calm down," Kai-lan says. The reel moved fast, with quick cuts and propulsive music designed to appeal to the adults in the room. It flashed on scenes with all the characters, including one in which they all counted to three in Mandarin. "Super counting!" Kai-lan cries.

When the lights came back up, producer Mary Harrington and creator Karen Chau were seated onstage, dressed stylishly and appearing composed. Harrington had been through press tour many times, but this was Karen's first exposure to it. Johnson served up questions from the audience, of which there would be time for just three. The first was about children's television's track record on diversity. Chau tackled it readily, noting the effusive support the show got when clips were brought to an Asian-American film festival in New York. "There was so much excitement when people saw this being represented." Another writer asked a similar question about why Mandarin had been chosen, given how difficult it is for most Westerners to learn. The group replied that they hadn't exactly gone language shopping; Chau's personal story and character menagerie happened to be Chinese; ergo, the show used Chinese.

Then a woman in the back fired off a thornier question, which was really more of a rant about today's parents flouting the American Academy of Pediatrics' recommendation for no TV before age two. "The reality is that most moms today are Gen Xers," the woman said. "They use media to get them through the day." Why, she wondered, is Nickelodeon effectively acting as their pushers? Johnson, Harrington, and Chau seemed a bit taken aback, but thankfully the format of the day allowed the question to linger only for a few seconds. They would have their brief rebuttal and that would be that. "We're trying to create the best content we can," Harrington said. "Every moment is vitamin-enriched." The woman pressed her point: "But some critics say it takes away from children's imagination." Johnson disagreed, but after a few seconds she was cued to turn things over to the next network to present, CMT.

Bob Kusbit, CMT's head of development, affected a brassy style diametrically opposed to that of the preschool crowd. His prey was the red-meat-eating adult male demo. He offered a terse acknowledgment: "Thank you, Brown. That's great stuff. Hard to follow up." But follow up he did, with Ty Murray's bull-riding show and a panel of celebrity guests, among them Vanilla Ice, and another series that went behind the scenes with the Dallas Cowboys Cheerleaders. "You might be thinking the headline of this story is, 'Cheers and Steers,'" he cracked. And with that one remorseless pun, *Ni Hao* had officially been erased from the press tour stage.

In the "greenroom" where VIPs gather before and after their turn on the dais, the Nick Jr. group was still flummoxed by the woman's diatribe, which had subverted the promotion of the show to some degree. Still, they felt glad the show had finally been sent, like a kindergartner, off into the world. Standing in a small circle next to Johnson, Harrington told me she sensed the show was going to be able to find some traction among parents who had adopted Chinese kids. "I've been doing a lot of reading on that community and have also spoken with people who—"

Jodi Davis, the irrepressible Nick Jr. publicist, broke in with an update on what was happening onstage. "Brown, it's the cheerleaders!"

All the women who were there for *Ni Hao* hurried into the back of the ballroom. Onstage, sure enough, were twelve Dallas Cowboys Cheerleaders, doing a full-tilt, high-kicking routine. It went on for almost five minutes. The women responsible for *Ni Hao, Kai-lan*, a show about a little girl who would guide millions of other little girls, stood admiring the cheerleaders. When they ended their routine with a physics-defying full split, the crowd went wild. "We had heard about this during the run-through, but we had to see it," Davis said.

The fleeting press tour appearance, with its deliberate staging and tightly edited video, presented a buffed and polished image of *Ni Hao, Kai-lan*. The reality was a little different, as the creative team battled to meet its deadline. Not long before press tour, Nick Jr. had assessed the situation and decided to delay the debut of the show from late August to late October. Even making that October deadline was no guarantee.

Kay Wilson Stallings, the executive at Nick Jr. overseeing *Ni Hao*, said the decision to postpone was not a difficult one. "When we launch a show, we aim to have ten episodes ready," she said.

"We usually 'strip' them, meaning we run ten new ones right out of the gate. With *Ni Hao,* even if all the stars were aligned, we would have had six to eight." The network also had its hands full with a major launch of the show *Yo Gabba Gabba!,* which was looking like a hit with big-league merchandising potential. Fueled by a hip-hop-flavored soundtrack and an off-kilter visual sensibility, the show had been championed by Johnson. Aggressive plans were being made for selling *Yo Gabba* consumer products around the world as well as securing TV deals everywhere possible. Appearances on the show by guests such as Elijah Wood, Devo co-founder Mark Mothersbaugh, and indie rock band The Shins offered many promotional hooks.

Wilson Stallings and Harrington kept returning to the same realization. "Unlike with other series, we didn't do a pilot," Wilson Stallings said. "We didn't have that foundation, so we were developing and producing at the same time." Agreed Harrington, "Our progress was hurt by not doing a pilot. We could have tested a lot more things earlier." There were a couple of reasons behind the rare, though not unprecedented, decision to skip the pilot phase. Nickelodeon, mindful that *Blue's Clues* was in its twilight, needed to keep new shows moving through the pipeline. The concept behind *Ni Hao* also was so appealing and timely that when executives weighed their options, a pilot seemed like an extra step that could eat up valuable time. Ironically, the decision only created longer delays. Even so, Wilson Stallings struck an upbeat note. "The research is a good guide," she said. "We know from storyboards how things are shaping up."

And the feedback told them plenty of positive things. But the bar had been set rather high in terms of execution. More complex than even the early days of *Dora,* when writers had to match up Howard Gardner's multiple intelligences with Spanish phrases,

Ni Hao had four curricular aspects that each script and each piece of animation had to take into account: socio-emotional, interactive, Chinese culture, and Chinese language.

Revising scripts and mastering the structure certainly was a full-time job, and as episodes entered production in 2007 the international flow of the animation work also proved a little cumbersome. Harrington described a number of "retakes," for either creative or technical reasons. Sometimes the colors—one of the show's visual trademarks—didn't come out quite right. Or the character's eyes were not looking directly at the viewer during those crucial interactive moments.

By the summertime, Sascha Paladino had been given an important bump. He had been awarded a producer credit to go with his status as head writer, a major opening for creating his own shows in the future. But with so few episodes "locked," or finished with all elements of production, he was not finding much time to celebrate. As consultants scrutinized each moment of each episode for the culture and language components—probably the chief element on which the show would be judged initially—a feeling set in that the writers and producers, who, except for Chau, lacked experience with Chinese, needed some more expert guidance. So they brought in a native speaker named Simon Sun as a language consultant with a screenwriting background. After moving to the United States at age twenty-five, he had attended film school at the University of Southern California and had a script accepted by an elite laboratory program at Sundance in Colorado. "We couldn't decide where was an appropriate place to put Chinese because we don't know Chinese," Paladino said. "He would read scripts and say, 'Here we could add a couple sentences' and that helped us stay on track." As casting was completed and actors came in to record, that also required adjustment. "You don't really know at first who is going to be really strong when they record and how that can change the emphasis of certain lines," Paladino said.

Music brought other final-stage challenges. While the show had always been conceived with some short musical asides, the appetite for music as a promotional tool, as well as the role it could play in helping the show emphasize its emotional curriculum, meant that music became a bigger consideration as 2007 progressed. The writers and producers wanted the musical moments to be as memorable to the audience as those in *Blue's Clues* or *Wonder Pets!* providing curricular takeaways that kids would actually look forward to.

In keeping with the recent preschool trend that has seen They Might Be Giants write the theme song to *Mickey Mouse Clubhouse,* Nickelodeon reached out to a musician who could bring a pop sensibility to the preschool world—Matt Mahaffey, the Tennessee-born center of a mid-'90s collective known as Self, which combined Beatles-esque guitar melodies with shambling, electro-hip-hop rhythm tracks. He had also toured as a member of Beck's band and, owing partly to Self's record deal at DreamWorks, wrote a song ("Stay Home") that was featured in the first *Shrek* movie. Mahaffey's theme song for *Ni Hao* was a sugar-rush track with techno cymbals and soaring vocals ("Kai-laaaaaan. . . . Ni hao! . . . Kai-laaaannn") and a synthesized beat that would not be out of place in a Shanghai disco. Under the glittery track, Paladino's lyrics highlight the emotional themes of the show. "I show my friends / how much I really care / So when someone needs my help / I'll always be right there." Other musical moments during episodes, which had come across as a capella in animatics tests and earlier cuts of episodes, blossomed into fully orchestrated passages driven by keyboard melody lines and propulsive beats. "When you feel too mad," Kai-lan sings to Rintoo, who was infuriated by finishing last in the dragonboat race, "the first thing you do . . . is calm . . . calm . . . down." Rintoo responds: "I got it, I got it. It's really, really true. I got it, I got it. I know just what to do." Happily, the voice actors can all carry a tune. "We hadn't cast them based on singing ability because we had no idea there would be this much music," Harrington said.

After Labor Day, with *Yo Gabba Gabba!* established as a strong newcomer, those charged with launching *Ni Hao, Kai-lan* realized that not enough episodes were ready. They were still short of the magic minimum of ten. Six weeks before the scheduled October 22 debut, the premiere was not locked and therefore could not be sent out to help draw media attention or build awareness among parents. An April feature story in the *New York Times* arts and leisure section, a publicity coup originally timed to prime readers for the show's August debut, was quickly losing resonance. Given the state of production, however, Nickelodeon decided the only logical move was to postpone the launch again— the fourth schedule change in the show's history. After some internal discussion, executives settled on mid-February 2008, around Presidents' Day and Chinese New Year, as the proper platform. "We realized we were overly ambitious," Wilson Stallings said in October. "We were backing into a date. February seemed like a stronger time of year. There was a lot of noise on our air in the fall and this way, especially with the Chinese New Year, it makes it look very deliberate that we timed it this way." Harrington also said the publicity potential around Chinese New Year was enticing. "It's going to be 4706, the year of the rat," she noted. "I think that's supposed to be a good year."

Given her connections, my daughter, Margot, would not have to wait until February to get her first look at *Ni Hao, Kai-lan*. She had enjoyed the *Downward Doghouse* shorts, and in October saw a rough cut of "Dragonboat Festival," which was originally conceived as the kickoff episode. (It was replaced, for obvious thematic reasons, by "Happy Chinese New Year!")

Conditioned by my investigation of the preschool business, I certainly spotted in *Ni Hao* some of the telltale marks of the Nickelodeon machine. The interactive moments as well as the multicolored outdoor backgrounds brought *Dora* immediately to mind. The music was such a prominent feature that the more contemplative, yogic feel of the early incarnations had been punched up significantly. Even so, the root characters and sensibility that had prompted Harrington's interest years earlier remained remarkably intact. Karen Chau's bits of inspired whimsy were still there—as Rintoo is learning to calm down and cope with his angry feelings, a trio of ducks in grass skirts doing a hula dance (called the Hula Ducks, naturally) appear out of nowhere. A dragon rises magisterially out of the water. Lulu the pink rhino not only floats around suspended from a red balloon, but an owl called Howard sits on his head, like a symbiotic tickbird on the back of an actual rhino. That kind of free-form expressiveness is a rare thing in preschool.

The DVD provided by Nickelodeon was designed to play the episode over and over again in a continuous loop. I started out watching with Margot, only to start reading the paper as she remained glued. (Some things never change.) By the time I looked up, the episode had started again. She would have watched a third time if I hadn't interceded and I recalled those many mornings on our living room floor when she started to whine and protest. "Kai-lan! Daddy, I want more Kai-lan!" The reason for her instant ardor wasn't clear, nor was it guaranteed to remain through multiple viewings. But she was certainly hooked. I looked over as the second showing concluded and asked her whether she understood the part about being angry, the lesson about how calming down was a crucial step in dealing with anger. She nodded absently, eyes fixed on the screen. I thought of that reaction later when Paladino told me about constructing the cornerstone moment of each episode, when Kai-lan, aided by a thought bubble and frame-within-frame animation, reflects on what happened to a character, what emotion it evoked, and what the resolution was. "Thinking is not very preschool," Paladino said. "That was one of the huge challenges we went through. How do you make that moment exciting? I thought about using chalk, having Kai-lan diagram it like a football play. But we ended up with something a little more restrained." In earlier versions, it was multiple choice—should the character have chosen A, B, or C? It later became more of a yes-no question, asking the child viewer to weigh in on whether the character did the right thing, leading him or her to the conclusion. "It's not perfect," Paladino said of the show overall, "but we managed to hit a lot of our goals. We did twenty episodes and we have language, we have culture, we have intergenerational relationship." Harrington, who has worked on countless animated shows in her career, said the 2–5 demo was "unquestionably the hardest and smartest crowd to reach. Can you believe that?"

The language component will likely draw the most attention, at least initially. It was hard to tell how successful that aspect was in our household, at least based on some highly unscientific initial research. At four, Margot had reached that amazing age when dinnertime conversations can often be dominated by questions about how to spell every word she can think of. I quizzed her the night she had watched *Ni Hao* for the first time about a couple of Mandarin words. She was fuzzy on it and couldn't fill in the blanks when I said, "How do you say, 'one, two, three'?" (I remembered the exchange in the very first focus group I attended in Glendale: "How do you say 'hat' in Chinese?" "Hat in Chinese.")

Academic research is also inconclusive on language acquisition through media—one University of Connecticut study in 2000
found no correlation between educational TV (such as *Sesame
Street*, which has contained a lot of Spanish for decades) and language development. Patricia Kuhl at the University of Washington also looked specifically at Mandarin learning—among babies,
admittedly a different audience from *Ni Hao's*—and found a big
gap between what they could learn from live instructors versus
the same instruction shown to them on DVD. Wilson Stallings
was convinced, based on the extensive research the network had
compiled, that there was room to add much more Mandarin to
future episodes. "If anything, we might do more language," she
said. "There is already an episode toward the end of season one
where full sentences are used. They teach how to say 'my name is'
and phrases like that."

Back in mid-August, just as *Ni Hao, Kai-lan* was navigating
the hectic homestretch, Nickelodeon had made an announcement
whose wide impact was not diminished by the fact that it had long
been expected. Noggin, the successful channel for preschool kids
that began a decade ago as a joint experiment with Sesame Workshop, was becoming its own twenty-four-hour cable channel. As
of December 31, 2007, it would no longer split the day in two and
share it with teen channel The N. The jargon-laden official press
release said the move was "part of MTV Networks' niche programming strategy to super-serve targeted audiences."

The financial results certainly justified the move. Revenues at
the combined Noggin-N channel had risen fourfold from 2002 to
2006, to $110.2 million. Investment in programming had more
than doubled in that time, to $31.9 million from $15 million. All
signs pointed to a sustainable round-the-clock model. The move
was likely to send the numbers even higher, to persuade more peo-

ple in the business world that the youngest demographic is also the fastest-growing and the most prized for what it can deliver: moms and an entire generation of kids. If Noggin was "like preschool on TV" and modeled after a typical day at an actual preschool, how would they fill time slots like 10 P.M. or 2 A.M.? Would they, like PBS Kids Sprout, have a "Good Night Show" and, as with the BBC, a "Morning Zone" for preschoolers? Perhaps a midnight movie and some infomercials could be worked in. Then again, I thought of all of those night wakings, those road trips, those moments where parents crave an anytime playdate. In 21st-century America, a round-the-clock Noggin, like supermarkets that never close, was inevitable—almost an inalienable right.

12

"TIME TO GO"

Dreaming of a Televised Future

The brick building in lower Manhattan where an increasing amount of preschool TV comes to life dates to 1790, when New York was becoming the shipping capital of America. Boats would dock on the East River just north of the financial district to unload goods into warehouses lining the port. The four-story structure at 207 Front Street (a cobblestone stretch so named because it once fronted the river) still has many of the features of its earliest incarnation as a granary, when grain just off ships was stored, processed, and prepared for distribution to a hungry new nation. A giant wheel made of dark wood stretches eight feet in diameter on the building's top floor, next to a shaft that runs the length of the building. Both features are original to the building, as are the low, wood-beamed ceilings and brick fireplaces that remain intact. For the previous forty years, the building was the home of the South Street Seaport Museum.

Josh Selig offered some of this historical context as he guided me around the building, which recently became the headquarters of the company he founded in 1999, Little Airplane. The force behind *Wonder Pets!*, a highly successful new show on Nickelodeon that brought a new animation technique called "photo puppetry" to preschool TV, it has other credits, including *Oobi*, an early Noggin show that used Señor Wences–style human hand puppets with Ping-Pong ball eyes, and a series of shorts on the Disney Channel called *Oh Baby.*

In many respects, Selig can be considered the heir to the 21st-century preschool TV throne. As the proprietor of a robust independent operation with more than sixty employees and the ability to produce programs from end to end—research to scripts to animation to puppet making to sound recording all under one historic roof—he is in a unique position to lay down a blueprint for how preschool is done. Little Airplane convenes twice-yearly "academies" to school any paying customer who's interested. A Manhattan native, Selig was a child actor on *Sesame Street* and eventually, after studying poetry at Sarah Lawrence College, returned to the show for a ten-year stint as a writer, producer, and filmmaker. Selig personifies the changes that have marked the preschool landscape over the past forty years. His appearances on *Sesame Street* as a young child "scarred me for life," he joked in one interview. "My childhood was a blur of furry monsters, alphabets, and googly eyes. I thought Hooper's store was a real store, and I was confused when they wouldn't take my money. I had no other choice but to pursue a career in children's television."

During the Sesame Workshop years, he felt most at home making his own short films, the ones about the alphabet, numbers, or playing pretend. One, called "I'm a Little Airplane," provided the name of his company. In spite of the immeasurable experience he gained from the show, he was always bound for an independent life.

Although the end of his run was less than harmonious, for reasons that will be addressed in a moment, when Selig told me he considers *Sesame Street* to be something of an endangered species, it got my attention. He noted that the PBS affiliate in Chicago decided to start airing half of the hour-long show (a decision since reversed) and says age compression has hit the show harder than most. Maybe "Elmo's World" will one day devour its host program, I suggested. He agreed it's a possibility. Selig also mentioned that Little Airplane had been negotiating with Fred Rogers's Family Communications to do the company's next show, its first since *Mister Rogers' Neighborhood* went off the air in 2001. If these events, or even less dramatic ones, did come to pass and *Wonder Pets!* kept on being *Wonder Pets!*, Selig would be an even more significant figure in preschool than he is today.

Selig's blue eyes, unwavering gaze, and implacable demeanor make him resemble a cross between Greg Kinnear and New England Patriots coach Bill Belichick, a good combination for an independent business owner. Even so, he quickly tired of my business-oriented questions about DVD sales, merchandise, overseas rights. My mistake seemed to have been assuming that the smooth company president who showed me around each cranny of the company headquarters and explained how all the parts fit together would also be interested in offering a tour of the company balance sheet.

"I don't know the answers to these questions because I'm not a businessman," he said, showing a fiery side for the first time in a two-hour visit. "I am not in this for the money. I don't have a lot of money. If I wanted to make money, I would go to L.A. like everybody else. I am in this industry because it gives a little window in a child's life, a chance to communicate something good to them as they're being inundated and bombarded with commercial messages and product pitches, more so than in any civilization in history."

We've been sitting outside having lunch in South Street Seaport, which was made over in the 1980s into a shopping mall with restaurants along the docks, where a few preserved tall ships from centuries ago draw crowds of tourists. Wherever there are tourists in New York, there are sure to be street performers, and indeed a handful of them worked the seaport as we ate. As a juggler and comedian in his early twenties, Selig would set up his props outside Broadway theaters and do a precisely honed, seven-minute act for tips. No matter how big a player he gets in a business sense, he wants to preserve the creative core of his company. Google, he said for emphasis, "may not look like an artist colony to you, but it is to me."

While that worldview seems entirely consistent with a nonprofit like Sesame, Selig had, by the end of his run, tired of its fundamentally bureaucratic nature. The end was hastened when he wrote an op-ed piece for the *New York Times* describing an extraordinary project he had personally overseen for the Workshop: a version of Sesame Street jointly produced by Israel and Palestine. The piece was edited without Selig's approval, he says, to emphasize the Palestinian part of the show, which was more of a novelty. The top executives at Sesame felt undermined by the way the piece came out, and claimed he hadn't given them sufficient advance notice that he was even writing it, which Selig says was also false. "I was offended by people feeling they could control my voice," he said. Several people at Sesame said Selig is still regarded as a controversial figure, but they all acknowledged the success of Little Airplane and, in fact, Sesame recently hired the company to produce a bible for a series in development.

In more than one interview, Selig has declared that people "peak at age four," that those early years of vivid, unchecked imagination and lack of boundaries is something he has always wanted to bottle. He has no kids of his own (yet) but he has Little Airplane. The company does not operate with the rigorously educational focus of other production houses in the preschool world. It tests only the early versions of episodes once, in storybook form, never animatics, and does not strictly adhere to the CTW Model. "When I'm creating a new show, I just go with my instincts," he once told the Web site Gothamist. "I try not to over-think it. Thinking can kill any good idea. Certainly all the networks do a lot of focus-group testing, but I think everyone takes those results with a grain of salt. After all, making TV shows is not a science."

During our interview, he expanded on that idea. "Preschoolers by and large are not drawn to things that are very high-tech," he said. "There's kind of an evergreen quality to what interests them. Going to the park, birthday parties, the beach. The themes that were there twenty to twenty-five years ago. Keeping up with clothes and music and trends has never interested me. Popular culture has never held any appeal for me. Within the domain of preschool, the look and the way we're executing the animation might change, but the core stuff is the same stuff.

"I have very clear memories of being a child and that was a really happy time for me. When I'm generating a new idea, I am responding to it on that level, like would I want to see three animals get into this vehicle called a flyboat and go to Africa or China [as the main characters do on Wonder Pets!]. That to me sounds exciting. That part of my mind is still active."

He had mostly maintained steady eye contact, but for a moment he looked away, out toward the water. I asked him how he sees himself fitting into the bigger picture, an increasingly competitive and gray landscape of age compression and merchandising and ever higher stakes.

"I don't see myself doing preschool my whole life, but for now it's where I've made my mark," Selig said. "It's a very specialized area driven by people wanting to get all those licensing dollars. They get into it in a very cavalier way. They think they can just saunter into the preschool market and come up with a show that kids will like. You have a lot of companies spending a lot of money to make really bad shows or have bad development and not even getting shows on the air. Someone who's in this for the dollars shouldn't get into preschool or babies. They should go to Hollywood. Fortunately, those people don't succeed that often. At Sesame, I often experienced situations where the creative people and the businesspeople were at odds. I never want that for my company. I want the businesspeople and the creative people to be the same. I may grow to the point where I say, 'I don't really want to make this show, but the businesspeople say it will sell,' but I'd rather go out of business. I'd rather go back to being a writer. They wince at their own shows. They're saying, 'Well, that's all we had the budget to do' and making excuses for their work and I never want to do that with my company."

I returned to Little Airplane a few days later to observe a focus group for season two of *Wonder Pets!* It was conducted by the company's head of research, Laura Brown, who is also a consultant for *Ni Hao, Kai-lan* and worked on shows like *Blue's Clues* and *The Backyardigans,* as well as on *Baby Einstein* videos. Four kids were there, aged three through five, but because one was an older sibling only three kids' opinions were being recorded. The test was far less formal than the tests I had seen for *Ni Hao* because *Wonder Pets!* does not feature the interactive devices of *Blue's Clues* or *Dora* or *Little Einsteins.* In a small room separated from the reception area by a red velvet curtain, the kids sat on an Oriental rug in a tight cluster around Brown, who had a script in her lap and a storybook with illustrations in the other. The children's mothers sat in chairs a few feet away.

The script had been through just one revision, and the artwork was very preliminary. This level of storybook testing was typically as far as the focus-group process goes on *Wonder Pets!* Because of its curriculum, which mainly encourages collaboration and problem-solving, there usually isn't a need to make sure that the precepts are being understood. Once the pets have been fully "cute-ified," as the company's employees sardonically put it, they are left to do their stuff.

Brown does a couple of interesting things as she conducts the focus groups: she sings and occasionally affects a speech impediment. The show is written as an operetta, with music recorded weekly in the Little Airplane building and the pint-size singers recorded in a neighboring room. One of the three main characters, Ming-Ming, can't pronounce her *r*'s, so Brown follows suit. She speeds through the story—titled "Kalamazoo"—about a visit by Ming-Ming to her cousin, Marvin, who is just a little chick. Ming-Ming is put in charge of Marvin, but finds that, as grown-up as she feels, she isn't used to the responsibilities of taking care of a little one.

The episode marks a major departure, in that Tuck and Linnie do not appear and the trio's famous flyboat is never flown. Instead, the focus is squarely on Ming-Ming and Marvin, and I soon learn why: Nickelodeon and Little Airplane are trying to come up with a spin-off show and this episode offers a potential route to it. The instantaneous success of *Go, Diego, Go!*, which was spun off from *Dora* in 2006, has shown Nick that looking to existing shows is safer than taking chances on new ideas from the start.

As Brown reads the script, the quartet of kids occasionally interrupts her. "How did they fly there?" one asks. "Corn? I love corn!" shouts another. Brown is unfazed. "You do? I do, too," she says. They generally remain focused and quiet as she reads.

Once the reading is done, Brown starts in with a series of questions. She's polished enough that they seem casual and conversational. The first few test general comprehension. What was the story about? Why was it hard for Ming-Ming to take care of Marvin? What happened at the end of the story?

The kids are all adorable, sometimes exasperating, but always, refreshingly, just preschool kids. They all rate the episode highly, though they were confused about some of the plot setup about Marvin and his relationship to the Wonder Pets. But based on her preliminary findings, Brown's report to Nickelodeon is that the spin-off show could fly.

In his classic education text *Emile*, Jean-Jacques Rousseau wrote that "reading is the scourge of childhood, for books teach us to talk about things we know nothing about." Taking it further, Neil Postman argues, "In a literate world children must become adults. But in a non-literate world there is no need to distinguish sharply between the child and the adult, for there are few secrets, and the culture does not need to provide training in how to understand itself." I kept wondering, while investigating baby/preschool entertainment, whether this booming industry was helping gradually to erode our notions of a literate society. Postman, the critic known for books such as *Amusing Ourselves to Death,* prefers the term "post-literate" in his essential polemic *The Disappear-*

ance of Childhood. The book outlines how the concept of childhood first evolved during the Enlightenment before an "uncoordinated but powerful assault on language and literacy" occurred in the 19th and 20th centuries. The result: beyond KGOY, it is nothing less than the end of the idea of kids, with adults dressing like children and vice versa, and the pressures and seductions of adulthood setting in younger and younger. "Most people no longer understand and want the traditional, idealized model of the child because that model cannot be supported by their experience or imagination," Postman writes.

What new child is the media-saturated 21st century and its exponents, such as Little Airplane, creating? Friends and fellow parents would often ask me to offer a bottom-line assessment that resulted from my research. "So, what did you find out? Is TV good or bad for kids?" I thought by this point I would have The Answer, a neat narrative arc describing the impact of TV on preschoolers and a corresponding code of behavior that I would introduce to my family. But the either/or proposition seems, increasingly, to be false in the face of so many choices. I found myself engrossed by Postman but not totally convinced that he was 100 percent right.

When I mentioned *The Disappearance of Childhood* to a friend, the writer Alissa Quart, whose last book examined gifted children, she dismissed it for hewing too closely to the leftist orthodoxy that considers technology a force of destruction that is sending the world toward chaos. She posits that a visually oriented society may not be such a bad thing, that kids who are more visual are typically just as smart, maybe even more so, than kids who spend more time reading. In a similar vein, Leonard Shlain, a theoretician and surgeon, has argued convincingly that screen images are reordering the contemporary brain in a way that will make print words irrelevant—a blessing, he believes, given the centuries of misogyny and repression that the alphabet has enabled.

If there are any people working in preschool TV who would likely reject those ideas outright, they are probably to be found on the fourteenth floor of an anonymous skyscraper between Manhattan's Times and Herald squares. This is where some of the main brains behind *Blue's Clues* have mobilized for a new preschool TV challenge. There, production company Out of the Blue, founded by *Blue*'s creator Angela Santomero and longtime Nickelodeon executive Samantha Freeman, has been ramping up a major new series premiering on PBS at the same time as *Ni Hao, Kai-lan*. Called *Super Why!*, it is billed as a superhero literacy show for kids ages three to six. Its 3-D-animated protagonists help solve typical preschool dilemmas by traveling inside books (not unlike the way Blue once "skidooed" into a painting) to find solutions. Instead of the clues scribbled down in the "handy dandy notebook," the puzzles embedded within each *Super Why!* episode are designed to teach spelling, reading, and comprehension. Having popularized interactive television and shown that watching it makes kids smarter, Santomero, Freeman, and *Blue*'s researcher Alice Wilder have set the bar much higher with *Super Why!*

Spending a day with Out of the Blue on a research expedition and debrief helped me see why their show has the potential to add some thrust to the educational component of preschool TV. The main reason is an explicit commitment to detailed research, which comes partly from the child development backgrounds of Santomero and Wilder and partly from the rigor that results from the show's funding by a Department of Education grant. Instead of one or two adults, as in the other shows' focus groups I had observed, there were four researchers, broken into teams of two.

They simultaneously tested slightly different versions of the same episode, number thirty-nine out of the series' unusually large sixty-five-episode initial order, to help ensure comprehension and interactivity scores.

The site for the research was the Acorn School, a private preschool whose students are mostly white and from higher-income families. The show has been tested all over—various socioeconomic strata in neighborhoods stretching from New Jersey to Queens, Connecticut to lower Manhattan. Even though it's intended for kids no older than six, *Super Why!* has been tested on nine-year-olds with remedial reading ability, who sparked to the superhero theme even as they struggled to follow the portions involving spelling and sentence structure. *Super Why!* also tested at a school called the IDEAL School of Manhattan (Individualized, Differentiated Education for All Learners), known for its advanced program for learning-disabled kids.

The *Super Why!* test I observed was a storybook test, but involved probably triple the number of pages of the test for *Ni Hao, Kai-lan*. Wilder sat cross-legged in front of three different groups of four to five kids each. The session took place in a large classroom, so the noise of a typical preschool day—singing, reading aloud, and laughing—was constant. Wilder was clearly at ease in the setting. She has probably, by her own reckoning, done more than one thousand of these sessions.

Compared with other moderators I had seen in action, Wilder was far more demonstrative, pointing to the page to underscore objects, scrolling through letter choices, and generally guiding the kids' attention. Instead of just following the script dialogue, she would detour to ask, "Where's the R?" passing the pages around so that everyone could find it. Occasionally, she scribbled notes on the script in a red pen. She and her assistant, who took notes continuously, read from a version of the episode's script that wove in the focus-group questions.

Like *Blue's Clues,* each episode of *Super Why!* follows a set structure, with a few so-called "formal features"—that is, the Thinking Chair or Mail Time. The Super Readers, the central quartet of superheroes, meet in the Book Club after being summoned, along with the viewer, with a question-mark beam that lights up the skies over Storybrook Village as the Bat signal does Gotham City. The Super Readers convene before the Super Computer, at the center of a meeting area tucked into packed bookcases that appear to stretch on forever. The oversize computer screen replays a video illustrating the information challenge confronting the superheroes, and they reach a decision about which book to consult for answers. The book is brought down from the shelf, the characters jump into it, and they immediately start interacting with the book's characters and scrutinizing its text. In one episode, for example, just by changing a few words, the "big bad wolf" becomes the "small good wolf," and a threat is neutralized.

After the day at Acorn, the team returned to the Out of the Blue offices, laying out stacks of sixteen-page research summaries on a conference room table. Once the data and videotape had been reviewed, a single document will summarize the day at Acorn School. The documents contain comments such as "Going up the stairs was a big moment. Research recommends that we play it up," or "Researchers noted that kids especially liked" a long list of things. "Literacy is such a hot button that we definitely expect some people not to like what we're doing," Wilder said. "So that's why we have to be committed to research because it will point us to what really gets through to kids. After *Blue's Clues,* that's just built in to our process. I didn't necessarily want to work on another show and I turned a lot of things down, but this seemed like an opportunity I couldn't pass up."

As *Super Why!* neared the starting gate, across town, *Sesame Street* was gearing up for its thirty-ninth season. Because that was the first TV show Margot and I had ever seen, I thought my mission would not be complete until I paid a visit to the people charged with keeping the longest-running preschool series current. *Sesame Street* has a reputation for quality that few of its rivals share. But that now cuts both ways, as evidenced by the *Sesame Beginnings* misadventure. New parents like me see *Sesame Street* as the gold standard and expose their kids at earlier and earlier ages, which has wreaked a bit of havoc with the curriculum.

"Parents view us as a safe alternative," said Carol-Lynn Parente, head of production at Sesame. "The alarming part about that is that a two-year-old cannot benefit from the show's design. And the curriculum is wasted on them." As a result, she continued, "We're reviewing what we do in order to constantly address the needs of our target audience. We're really trying to hit the twos and threes."

One hallmark of *Sesame Street* is its "magazine format," which involves the blending of thirty-five to forty unique segments over the course of an hour. That format "was working almost too well for younger kids and the older ones have moved on," Sesame discovered. Also, just as Selig observed, Parente conceded, "We are an hour-long show in a half-hour world."

I asked Parente how long she thought the hour-long format would last, especially given the fact that the fifteen-minute "Elmo's World" segment had grown so popular.

"The show is thought of as a playdate, never as a show," she said. "It's a playdate in an inner-city neighborhood. Within the hour, we're focusing more. It's much more continuous than it used to be as far as story. A story is broken up and told over the course of the hour, interspersed with somewhat random but themed segments. We took a look at changing to less than an hour, but we're not just a letters and numbers show."

The idea for *Sesame Street* is to return to one of its core strengths: teaching kids how to deal with emotions. "That is easier for us because we have characters getting at those story lines."

Parente cited an example from the season just passed: Rosita and Zoe are playing. The show's newest character, Abby Cadabby, comes in and bonds with Zoe, but Rosita wanted to play tag. So they start to fight about it. They try to work it out themselves and then adults come in to help. The goal was to model conflict resolution.

Gary Knell, the charismatic CEO of Sesame Workshop, feels optimistic about season thirty-nine but he did not sugarcoat the challenges facing Sesame. The four "pillars" of preschool TV—license fees from broadcasters, international sales, corporate or government support, and merchandising—are all under assault, he said.

"*Dora* will die," he said, tracing a dive-bomber trajectory with his hand. "These shows usually get about five to six years where they're at their hottest point, where everyone loves them and buys their products, but not a lot of them last after that." It wasn't petty rivalry that prompted his premonition—he felt the odds were squarely against another show matching the thirty-plus-year reigns of *Sesame Street, Mister Rogers,* or *Captain Kangaroo.*

The environment children grow up in today has also shifted irrevocably, and not for the better, he said. "Technology dominating our culture is a bad thing," Knell said. "There is a new generation of parents who don't define things as technology. They're just *things*. They won't draw a distinction between the time they're using a device and the time when they are not. Parents are feeling overwhelmed by that shift . . . And if you think the marketplace is crowded now, we're entering a period where everybody is a producer and distributor thanks to the Internet."

Karen Hill-Scott, a veteran educational consultant who has worked on shows for Nick Jr. and the Disney Channel, is a mother and a grandmother. Watching her preschool-age grandchildren grow up in a world exponentially more media-saturated than her kids' has been eye-opening, she says. And the confluence of societal factors leaves her less than completely encouraged about the future. "This really is the era of the weak parent," she says. With the generation raising kids more apt to plan out their future and make their own fulfillment a priority, "the power these children are given is quite amazing." As an example, Hill-Scott said a family she spoke with recently had their five-year-old boy choose the make, model, and color of their new car. "The thing is, when you give them that kind of power, it gives a chance for good habit systems not to take." Indeed, the charter of many preschool shows seems to be empowerment. Chris Gifford, one of the creators of *Dora the Explorer,* says the show is addressed to "the least powerful members of society." Viewers in this age group are hungry for the message that they can do things, he explained, given their reality of needing help with almost every day-to-day task. That's commendable on its face, but when toddlers are empowered to sit in a shiny, high-tech cockpit, how will they know how to manipulate the controls and not end up in a nosedive? "When people say kids today are smarter, I disagree," Hill-Scott said. "They're just more exposed."

Anne Wood, a former schoolteacher from a northern England military town, created *Teletubbies* more than a decade ago. The show's 365 episodes proved revolutionary, by explicitly aiming at children as young as one. Its characters touched off controversy that still lingers because they had televisions in their tummies and spoke in monosyllabic gibberish that Wood contends was a realistic, relatable simulation of actual baby talk. Critics insisted the characters would harm viewers' adoption of language, and they blasted PBS for promoting the series to such young viewers.

Nearly five decades into a storied children's publishing and television career, Wood returned to British TV with *In the Night Garden*, a $30 million series that sets about to explore a heretofore untapped realm: sleep and dreams. The show stakes out an alternate world that exists between wakefulness and sleep. As with *Teletubbies*, there is less of a linear plot than a mood and an atmosphere. Set in a sunlit glen (painstakingly shot in high definition outside Stratford-upon-Avon), it brings together human-sized characters of various colors and imaginary languages, the main ones being Upsy Daisy, Makka Pakka, IgglePiggle, and the Tombliboos. With a touch of *Nutcracker* fantasy, each show brings all the characters together in one setting, which is called the night garden because IgglePiggle discovers it while sailing alone in a little boat on a starry night.

Over a live-action image of a small child's palm being caressed in a circular motion by an adult's hand, a soothing woman's voice begins to sing, as in a lullaby, "The night is black and the stars are bright and the sea is dark and deep . . ." and then the bracing diction of Shakespearean actor Derek Jacobi picks it up, continuing, " . . . but someone I know is safe and snug and they're drifting off to sleep. Round and round, a little boat no bigger than your hand, out on the ocean faraway from land. Take the sail down, light the little light. This is the way to the garden in the night."

I met Wood in the high-ceilinged dining room of London's posh Langham Hotel. Over supper and sauvignon blanc, we talked about her unorthodox path to the front ranks of preschool entertainment and her status as a cultural lightning rod. Her cardigan sweater and gentle handshake were counterbalanced by a Phyllis Diller–like hair flourish: an icing-like shock of white atop a layer of brown. Her round, button-like, deep-set eyes convey a quiet intensity. "I've been reading a lot of Kurt Vonnegut lately because I'm interested in people's last words," she said.

"It became clear to me that there was more anxiety than there used to be, more anxiety about raising children," Wood said. "Why it was, I don't know, the media, September 11, the awareness of terrorism. We live in really anxious times and children have picked up on this. There's a lot of tension around the bedtime thing."

The show has become perhaps the purest expression of the open-ended philosophy that had long existed at Wood's company, Ragdoll, which does not test its shows in conventional ways. Instead of "research," she pointedly uses the term "observation."

"We found out by watching children that children need time to reflect," she said. "If you take them walking across the platform at a railway station, you get a lot of pigeons in London and you'll get a child hanging back to watch the pigeons. The parent wants to catch the train, but all they want to do is stand and look at the pigeon. And that's what they need to be allowed to do. That's what you can do with television. You can watch for a long time. I have been known to say to the cameraman, 'Don't take your eye off that thing!' You leave it longer, longer, longer, longer and *I'll* cut it. They always say, 'Well, we've got that shot, let's move on.'

But what does it take, another thirty seconds or another minute? I want you to hold it longer."

Night Garden has been wildly popular in the United Kingdom since debuting on the BBC in March 2007. Ragdoll plans to produce one hundred episodes, fewer than the 365 it did of *Teletubbies,* but more than enough to give the show some longevity. Something is significantly different this time around, however: it is not at all clear whether an American TV network will commit to airing the show. PBS, which picked up *Teletubbies* and *Tots TV,* is in a different place than it was a decade ago.

"PBS will say it's not educational," Wood said, noting that many of its new shows (such as *Super Why!*) are funded through U.S. Department of Education Ready to Learn grants. "America is very important. It's a huge market. We get so many American shows here, it would be nice to send one back!" She laughed, but then her smile faded. The show had been a labor of love to produce, and the topic seemed both novel and important. But the American preschool landscape didn't seem to have room for it.

"They're always worried about the sixty other channels. It's such a shame," Wood said. "When you come in to *In the Night Garden,* it's very slow, with this wonderful Shakespearean actor, it's not about teaching. It's about respecting the child's right to be. And trying to understand the world from a child's perspective. . . . They have to be seen to be teaching. We are not teachers. We respect children's right to learn. That's different. *Night Garden* came from listening to the needs that were expressed, the tensions that were there."

Wood's philosophy had infuriated a lot of people over the years and her openness to the idea that one-year-olds could get something valuable from *Teletubbies* made her a target of a lot of criticism. I hadn't known what to expect when I arranged to meet her. But there was something about her approach that actually seemed quite sensible, especially as I put it in the larger context of my travels through the preschool wilderness. She puts the child at the center of things in such a way that it is hard for me to marshal significant objections. Yet debate still rages about *Teletubbies*. A 2005 study that looked in every three months on babies and toddlers aged between six and thirty months determined that those who watched *Teletubbies* knew ten fewer words at thirty months when compared with those who watched other programs. They were more prone to vocalizations than others in the study, but that didn't take the form of English words. "Children were unable to learn novel words when inserted into a *Teletubbies* clip," the authors concluded. "Multiple forms of input, including music, visual stimulation and language, were too complex to enable word learning."

Many of Wood's sternest critics will find more reason for consternation in *Night Garden*. Aside from Jacobi, few characters utter what could safely be called words. But the qualities that I have looked for in children's TV, from the time when I was a toddler to my time as a dad, all seem to be in place: high production values, an element of fantasy, and a pronounced tilt toward the child's perspective. There is no checklist of developmental concepts that have been injected into the show like vitamins into a loaf of bread.

Margot and I were recently watching Disney Channel's new show, *My Friends Tigger & Pooh*, which preschoolizes the classic Winnie the Pooh menagerie, inventing a new six-year-old girl, Darby, as the protagonist. Using computer animation, the show blatantly appropriates the interactive techniques of *Blue's Clues* and its progeny and seems intent on teaching lessons every couple of minutes. That busy quality drains much of the color from the

Hundred Acre Wood, and I felt it had to do with the schism at the heart of the show. One of Pooh's famous lines in A. A. Milne's books is this bit of advice: "Don't underestimate the value of Doing Nothing, of just going along, listening to all the things you can't hear, and not bothering."

Author Susan Gregory Thomas latches on to Pooh in *Buy, Buy Baby*, a diatribe against the larger consumer environment preying upon parents of young children. She uses Doing Nothing as a kind of nostalgia-tinged shorthand for kids not being plugged in as they are today. I would offer a slightly different interpretation. Doing Nothing, to me, doesn't have to mean dropping out or detaching entirely. It just means meeting a work of popular imagination halfway, embracing it even if it is not machine-tooled to feed your demographic.

Anne Wood's whole career has been based on that kind of core belief that children can come to a work of art, rather than having it come to them. That notion certainly has some precedent outside of preschool entertainment. David Riesman, in his classic sociology text *The Lonely Crowd*, describes a shift in America from "inner-directed" personality types to "other-directed" ones. Inner-direction, he explains, is characterized by self-sufficiency, shaping by tradition-minded elders and movement toward "generalized but inescapable goals." Other-direction is about having one's course defined by acquaintances and the mass media, which causes one's goals to change continually. Published at the dawn of the TV age, in 1950, the book has aged creakily in some respects but magnificently in others. Its focus is generally on adults, but a fascinating passage toward the end examines the idea of "freeing the child market" with a proposal that is something of a rhetorical gimmick but also a striking comment on consumer groupthink, especially considering it is more than half a century old. To "producers and advertisers addressing themselves to the child market," Riesman suggests "the experimental creation of model consumer economies among children." In this "everyday World's Fair," luxury goods would be available for purchase. "At this 'point of sale,' there would stand market researchers able and willing to help children make their selections but having no particularly frightening charisma or overbearing charm or any interest on the employer's side in pushing one thing rather than another. The point of these 'experiment stations' would be to reveal something about what happens to childhood taste when it is given a free track away from the taste gradients and 'reasons' as well as freedom from the financial hobbles of a given peer-group."

Like Riesman, Anne Wood wants to give children the opportunity to criticize and reshape the value of objects around them, to be allowed to dawdle at the train station and watch the pigeons. As she sees it, adults are encroaching on kids' last remaining autonomous space. "The older you get, life is not simple, especially with the complexities of the shared culture children inhabit and the whole 'kidult' thing. Adults are plugging into children's culture more often."

I told Wood that everyone I had spoken with about my book had demanded a bottom-line assessment about whether exposing babies and preschoolers to TV was good or bad. She replied, "To say is television good or bad is ludicrous. You might as well say, 'Is print good or bad?' We're talking about cultural experience. . . . This idea that we have in every aspect of life that it can be a quick fix. 'Tell me, is it good or bad so I can abdicate any responsibility I have for thinking about it.' It's sad, really."

Reflecting on her own roots, she added, "I come from very working-class people. Horizons were very narrow. The content on television, I firmly believe, can open windows and widen horizons for children who otherwise don't have those experiences. A lot of the comment comes from middle-class people. You have something totally innocent like *Teletubbies* and you get all these people coming out and trying to destroy its innocence. There's no room for that kind of innocence."

Wood recalled her childhood in the north of England. "You either became a nurse or a teacher," she said. "I passed up university for financial reasons. I was always interested in imaginative development, in where does imagination reside, where does consciousness reside?"

Those early years, the very stretch of time being scrutinized by pediatricians, child development experts, and TV networks, proved a grueling test for Wood. When she was three, her father went off to fight in World War II. Two brothers had died before she was born, and she was the lone child who survived. Her mother worked in the munitions factory. "I was raised by my grandmother, who had seven children, so I was well taken care of," she said. "It makes you tough. Looking back, it was good because I was never overprotected. You went out into the rough-and-tumble with the other kids. And the community looked after you. If you strayed, somebody would say, 'You shouldn't be up here, you should be over there where you belong!' Now, of course, people don't do that anymore. If you take an interest in a child who isn't your own, you are seen as some sort of sinister figure."

It isn't difficult to draw a line from Wood's own difficult childhood—a brief but unforgettable portion of our couple of hours together—straight to *In the Night Garden*. The lone, childlike figure in the boat, lowering the sail, submitting to the unknown waves. The redeeming sunshine of the garden, a secret world behind the hedge, a refuge from life's difficulties. I thought of Mister Rogers's Land of Make Believe, the empowering moshes of Milkshake.

I needed to see how Margot and I would experience this show, three years after our first voyage into the dark seas. As she watched, her breathing became heavier and deeper. It was late evening, after her bath but before bedtime. She sat in my lap, as she had done when she was much smaller, unable to talk, unable to do all the things she does now. Instead of the pop-culture heirloom of *Sesame Street,* I was introducing her to something brand-new. Halfway through the episode, Margot seemed soothed and attentive. She suddenly sat up and declared, "This show is my favorite." Of course, she says that of a lot of shows, but it indicated a connection.

Anne Wood, Josh Selig, Angela Santomero, and the people behind *Sesame Street* have a sense of idealism, even a utopian streak, and that energy allows me hope for the future. What little research exists on the effects of TV on the very young contains important clues about the importance of content, not just exposure. In other words, quality matters. It seems to me that instead of wringing hands over the steady decline of American civilization as manifest by *Little Einsteins,* parents need to recognize innovation and make quality their mantra. David Kleeman, executive director of the American Center for Children and Media, is a consultant for Prix Jeunesse, a foundation that sponsors a biannual festival billed as a "world-embracing movement for high-quality TV." Especially given how much more fixated American preschool shows are on education than other countries' programs, Kleeman says the goal should be "achieving balance. If a show is creative and engaging and also manages to teach kids something, that, to me, is a good situation." Or as the late, influential preschool TV researcher John Wright was fond of saying, "Marshall McLuhan appears to have been wrong. The medium is not the message. The *message* is the message!"

The closing minutes of *In the Night Garden* show each character settling down and going to sleep. The only one left is IgglePiggle, still wandering through the garden. Jacobi, the narrator, calls to him. "Who's not in bed? IgglePiggle's not in bed." He pauses as IgglePiggle faces the camera and waves a wave of surrender. "Don't worry, IgglePiggle. It's time to go." That last phrase has uncanny resonance, calling to mind the march upstairs at bedtime, the end of the playdate. With the magic of special effects, the garden melts into the stars and IgglePiggle is shown stretched out once again in his little boat, sleeping as it bobs in the vast sea.

Wood said that the closing sequence, meticulously designed in order to ease viewers' return to reality, is the first of any show she has produced that has elicited tears from children. "After we've lulled them into such a state of relaxation and whatever, they get terribly upset," she said. "I don't know if it's Derek Jacobi saying, 'Time to go.' I'm going to see him soon and I may ask, 'Sir Derek, could you give us another reading of that line?'" She chuckles lightly and then pauses. "It's like a much-loved toy taken away from them."

Margot has objected to many a toy being taken away, but she didn't cry at Sir Derek's farewell. When the boat finished sailing into the horizon, she rolled over and stretched. "Daddy, I want to go to sleep," she said. I wondered what kind of dreams she would have after seeing the show. Would her imagination be spurred to some kind of action as she slept, helping her tack on IQ points while her body rested? Is that the next frontier of entertaining preschoolers? More likely, *In the Night Garden* is a simple update of the bedtime story, a way of reassuring children through pure imagination and pretend play that they are safe.

I stayed on the couch, holding my daughter and two-month-old son, Finley, who had arrived as I was finishing this book. Stella and I had talked about what the effect of the book might be on him. What, if anything, would we do differently with him than we did with Margot? The *Night Garden* episode ended and the DVD menu popped up, offering a choice of two more. I could still hear the mellifluous theme song and Sir Derek's firm but soothing tone. *In the Night Garden* suddenly seemed like the only place I wanted to be.

As the show twinkled to life and the boat set sail again, Finley stirred in my lap. His head turned ever so slightly toward the screen.

NOTES

Three of the most valuable sources for this book live at my own address—namely my wife, Stella, and our two children, Margot and Finley. Trying to make sense of our family's experience with media, however, meant venturing well outside the household. I interviewed more than hundred people across many disciplines in Boston, Denver, London, Los Angeles, and New York over a two-year period, and visited animation studios, trades shows, corporate suites, archives, and classrooms. Unless cited in the main text or the following notes, quotations are from author interviews.

Chapter 1

Tiny Love product descriptions from a company promotional DVD and interviews conducted at American International Toy Fair in February 2007.

The size of the market for all entertainment products aimed at children from birth to five years old is difficult to precisely capture, especially given how many consumers are under the age of two and therefore not accounted for in official tallies. Also, there is the challenge of how to count sales from toys connected to such brands as *SpongeBob SquarePants* that are aimed at school-age kids but actually consumed by toddlers. My estimate of $21 billion, therefore, is a calculation that factors in revenues from television, DVD, live shows, music, and licensed toys and consumer products, as reflected in company SEC filings and trade-group reports. The figure was vetted by numerous experts who work in the children's entertainment business. The growth rate has been driven by DVD and consumer products sales. Throughout this chapter, I drew from articles assessing revenues and growth patterns of significant product lines and categories, including "Kids DVDs in a Growth Spurt," *USA Today*, April 4, 2005, "How Dora the Explorer Slew Barney," *Slate*, June 24, 2005, "Stage Shows for Kids: A Grown-Up Industry," *USA Today*, July 3, 2007, "In Tots' TV Shows, A Booming Market, Toys Get Top Billing," *Wall Street Journal*, Jan. 27, 2006, and "Bringing Up Baby," *Adweek*, Feb. 13, 2006. *Dora the Explorer* ratings are from Nielsen Media Research. Baby Einstein valuations came from founder Julie Clark during an interview with the author.

Notes

Material in this chapter also derives from "The Media Habits of Infants and Toddlers: Findings from a Parent Survey," a 2004 study by the group Zero to Three coauthored by Deborah S. Weber and Dorothy G. Singer; and "Zero to Six: Electronic Media in the Lives of Infants, Toddlers and Preschoolers," a Kaiser Family Foundation report by Victoria Rideout, Elizabeth A. Vandewater, and Ellen A. Wartella. Juliet B. Schor's incisive book *Born to Buy* (Scribner: New York, 2004) also proved a valuable resource. Interpretations of William Blake were shaped by Ben S. Bradley's insightful book *Visions of Infancy: A Critical Introduction to Child Psychology* (Polity Press: Cambridge, U.K., 1989).

Two books about young children, entertainment, and marketing that were published during the preparation of my book have distinctly different emphases than mine but were useful resources: Lisa Guernsey's *Into the Minds of Babes: How Screen Time Affects Children from Birth to Age Five* (Basic Books: New York, 2007), and *Buy Buy Baby: How Consumer Culture Manipulates Parents and Harms Young Minds* (Houghton Mifflin: Boston, 2007).

Chapter 2

The account of the start of *Downward Doghouse* is drawn from author interviews as well as "Cartoons with Heart . . . and a Little Mandarin," *The New York Times*, April 15, 2007. The history of Nickelodeon benefited from an interview with Geraldine Laybourne as well as essays in *Nickelodeon Nation: The History, Politics and Economics of America's Only TV Channel for Kids*, Heather Hendershot, ed., (New York University Press: New York, 2004); and Norma Odom Pecora's *The Business of Children's Entertainment*, (The Guilford Press: New York, 1998); "What Makes Nick Tick," *The Philadelphia Inquirer*, July 19, 1998; and "When Cable Went Qubist" on Ken Freed's online magazine Media Visions Journal. Craig Marin quoted on John Norris Brown's Web site Classic Nick. Useful characterizations of the landscape of children's entertainment in the 1980s and '90s also appear in James Steyer's *The Other Parent: The Inside Story of the Media's Effect on Our Children*, (Atria Books: New York, 2002).

Chapter 3

Descriptions of research conducted for baby and toddler programming were shaped by author interviews with several research consultants and academics, as well as accounts in *"G" is for Growing: Thirty Years of Research on Children and Sesame Street* (Lawrence Erlbaum Associates: Mahwah, N.J., 2001) and *Nickelodeon Nation*.

224

Notes

Chapter 4

Details about the creation and evolution of *Dora the Explorer* stem from author interviews with its principal figures and email exchanges with Howard Gardner, as well as secondary sources listed for Chapters 1 and 2. Sarah Kozloff's essay, "Narrative Theory and Television" appears in *Channels of Discourse, Reassembled: Television and Contemporary Criticism* (University of North Carolina Press: Chapel Hill, N.C., 1987). Albert Bandura wrote extensively about his theories of social learning, including in *Social Foundations of Thought and Action: A Social Cognitive Theory*, (Prentice Hall: Englewood Cliffs, N.J., 1985). Linebarger's study, co-authored by Dale Walker, is "Infants and Toddlers' Television Viewing and Language Outcomes," *American Behavioral Scientist*, January 2005.

Chapter 5

Information about children's television from the late-1940s through the late-1960s is generally sketchy and incomplete, but my numerous visits to New York's Paley Center for Media's vast library, especially its video collection, helped fill in some of the most important gaps. Along with extensive viewing of shows and archival material, this chapter draws from *Television Cartoon Shows: An Illustrated Encyclopedia, 1949 to 2003*, Second Ed., Hal Erickson, (McFarland: Jefferson, N.C., 2005), "It's Howdy Doody Time," September 29, 2004, by Jim Lewis on his Web site, Fig Tree Notes from Under the Fig Tree. Diagnoses of "TV tummy" were reported in *Time*, February 18, 1952. Bob Keeshan's quote is included in a history of *Captain Kangaroo* on online fan site TVParty.com.

Chapter 6

Material in this chapter derives from author interviews and a visit to Nickelodeon's animation studio in Burbank, California, in April 2006.

Chapter 7

The framework for this chapter was established after visits to American International Toy Fair in February 2006 and 2007, as well as a trip to a similar event, Licensing Show, in July 2006. Other sources included Eric Clark's book *The Real Toy Story: Inside the Ruthless Battle for America's Youngest Consumers* (Free Press: New York, 2007) and data from the Toy Industry Association and Anita Frazier of the research firm NPD Group. Background of Kay Kamen is found in Walt Disney Co. archive material as well as the Kansas State Historical Society. Sesame Workshop financials are from the organization's 2007 annual report. The legacy of Bernard Loomis was highlighted in a *New York Times* obituary dated June 6, 2006.

Notes

Chapter 8

The foundation for this chapter is a two-and-a-half-hour visit to Julie Clark's home in Centennial, Colorado I also interviewed executives at BabyFirst TV in Los Angeles and Baby TV in London.

Data on awareness of the American Academy of Pediatrics is from a 2004 survey of parents of children under two conducted by the Kaiser Family Foundation.

Videos of Rachel Barr's work at Georgetown are viewable at the Early Learning Project Web site, http://elp.georgetown.edu. One of the articles I consulted was Barr and Harlene Hayne's "Developmental Changes in Imitation from Television During Infancy," *Child Development* 70, No. 5 (1999), 1067–1081.

Dan Anderson's presentation at the Society for Research in Child Development conference was described to me by Rosemary Truglio at Sesame Workshop and then verified with other attendees. Details about Baby TV and BabyFirst TV are from in-person interviews and follow-ups with both companies.

Chapter 9

Material in this chapter is from first-hand observation and author interviews.

Chapter 10

The most comprehensive overview of preschool music to date is "Kindie Rock," Salon.com, June 24, 2006. I also consulted "Kid Rock," *New York Times Magazine*, April 2, 2006.

Chapter 11

Cable revenue figures are from an SNL Kagan report. Networks supply Kagan with data and generally accept use of them by the media. The numbers were also vetted by Nickelodeon.

Chapter 12

This chapter relied on Leonard Shlain's book *The Alphabet Versus the Goddess: The Conflict Between Word and Image* (Viking Penguin: New York, 1998) and Linebarger and Walker, "Infants' and Toddlers' Television Viewing and Language Outcomes."

ACKNOWLEDGMENTS

A s with parenting, writing about babies and toddlers is hardly a solitary process. In the two-plus years it took for this book to go from concept to what you hold in your hand, many people offered invaluable insights and guidance, both as sources and fellow travelers. So many, in fact, that I won't ever be able to name them all. But here goes.

Personal thanks too often get stuck at the bottom of lists, but the nature of this project demands a different order. At the very top is my gorgeous and kind-hearted wife, Stella, for not only being an amazing mother to our two children, Margot and Finley, but also for taking care of them while I took breaks from the battlefield to write and travel. The book and my belief in it derive from conversations we had at all hours, over wine and formula, taking stock of parenthood. The spirit of Margot and Finley animates these pages and I hope if I have created a monster, it is a thoughtful one, since Margot turned from the TV the other day and asked, "So, are you going to write about this show, Dad?" I also thank my parents, Carol and Phil Hayes, and my sister, Emily, who not only rooted me on (as they always have) but also agreed to sift through memories of their childhoods and mine. My sister- and brother-in-law, Alla and Bill Broeksmit, narrowly escaped raising their children in the Baby Einstein era, but nevertheless offered unstinting encouragement and hospitality.

Acknowledgments

My agent, David Kuhn, deserves much of the credit for the inception of this book. When I offhandedly mentioned my fascination with the topic, he pounced and, even better than pouncing, worked patiently with me to whip the material into book shape. Many thanks also to the indefatigable Billy Kingsland at Kuhn Projects.

My gratitude also goes to everyone at Free Press, especially my editor, Leslie Meredith, a curious thinker and careful reader who has nurtured the book with great aplomb. I have also been lucky to have Marissa Hajtler on the promotional front lines. Andrew Paulson and Donna Loffredo were steady and personable resources throughout the process.

I also extend thanks to *Variety*, notably my colleagues in New York. I am fortunate to count Peter Bart, our singular editor, as my friend. Along with Phyllis Fredette, Peter's support of the book has meant a great deal.

Unlike the ego-ridden Hollywood studio lots I have navigated in recent years, the great serendipity in exploring preschool media was that people who create or evaluate it actively welcome the interest of even neophytes like myself. The genial and knowledgeable Alice Wilder illuminated my path through the industry as well as academia. Her creative partner at *Blue's Clues* and *Super Why!* Angela Santomero, also graciously allowed me to look in on their new enterprise. Josh Selig and Laura Brown at Little Airplane welcomed me, too, and were very accommodating. For their time and thoughts, I also thank Anne Wood, Dorothy Singer, David Kleeman, Marjorie Kaplan, Ellen Lewis, Gary Knell, Alice Cahn, Michael Rich, and his entire team at the Center on Media and Child Health. Lisa Mathews and Mikel Gehl of Milkshake were generous, fun-loving, and serious in equal measure.

Acknowledgments

The people working on *Ni Hao, Kai-lan,* notably Sascha Paladino, Mary Harrington, and Karen Chau, as well as a host of people at Nickelodeon Preschool, especially Jodi Davis, Sharyn Traub, Brown Johnson, and Kay Wilson Stallings, merit special mention. They responded to my many questions and allowed me to be a fly on the wall over a lengthy period.

Friends, whether fellow parents or not, also made lasting contributions to this book by joining me in thinking efficiently about the vast world of baby and preschool entertainment. Thanks to Nicole Laporte and Ruth Rushfield, Ruth Kennison and David Hochman, Victoria Neznansky and Michael Grin, Valeria Susania and Jack Womack, Alexandra Shapiro and Adam Aron. I hope and trust that this list will grow as my children do.

DADE HAYES
October 24, 2007

INDEX

Index

Index

Index

Index

Index

Index

Index

Index

ABOUT THE AUTHOR

DADE HAYES is assistant managing editor of *Variety*. He runs the editorial operations of the New York office and writes about television, film, business, and publishing. He spent six years as a reporter and editor at *Variety* in Los Angeles.

In 2004, Hayes co-wrote *Open Wide: How Hollywood Box Office Became a National Obsession*. The book was praised in *The New York Times*, called "a classic" by *The Atlantic*, and featured in *The New Yorker* and on public radio's FreshAir.

Hayes was previously a senior editor at *Entertainment Weekly* and a reporter for the *Los Angeles Times* and Associated Press. His freelance writing has appeared in *TV Guide*, the *Boston Globe*, and *Premiere*.

He lives in Larchmont, New York, with his wife, Stella, daughter, Margot, and son, Finley.